Zero to Boston

Journal of a Rookie Marathoner: Year One

By Jeff Kendall

Publisher's Cataloging-in-Publication data

Names: Kendall, Jeff, author.
Title: Zero to Boston / by Jeff Kendall.
Description: Includes bibliographical references. | Southfield, MI: jeffwrites.org, 2016.
Identifiers: ISBN 978-1537308340 | LCCN 2016914865
Subjects: LCSH Kendall, Jeff. | Marathon running--Biography. | Marathon running--Training. | Boston marathon. | BISAC SPORTS & RECREATION / Running & Jogging | BIOGRAPHY & AUTOBIOGRAPHY / Sports | SELF-HELP / Motivational & Inspirational
Classification: LCC GV1065.17.T73 K46 2016 | DDC 796.42/52--dc23

Contents

Foreword

I began kicking around the idea of keeping a journal when I first picked up running again in 2015. Toward that end, I recorded everything in a google spreadsheet. I started out with simply distances, elapsed times and paces but as I learned more about running, I added columns and categories to track things like VO2max calculated from that day's performance and heart rate. This provided a wealth of information for me to draw upon as I reflect on making it from no running whatsoever to qualifying for the Boston Marathon in less than one calendar year. I considered stopping there but realized qualifying was really a midpoint in the story so I decided to continue my writing to cover the year leading up to Boston after I qualified.

#0toBoston

At first I was calling my story, "Couch to Boston, A Runner's Story" but my friend Tammy suggested "Zero to Boston" might work better. While I know runners will immediately recognize the "couch to…" title, "zero to…" is a bit more descriptive of my situation. I didn't quite go from couch to anything because I was pursuing some low impact fitness activities, but it is accurate to say zero to because my running before 2015 was almost exactly zero. I also changed the subtitle to "Journal of a Rookie Marathoner: Year One." and I also decided to start using the twitter hashtag... #0toBoston.

A marathon is primarily a mental activity. Most of the self discipline required takes place above the shoulders. My nephew Kyle studied exercise physiology and he shared with me that anything your body can do for half an hour (such as a 5K) it can do all day (such as a marathon). The trick is listening to your body without letting your body set the day's agenda. How do you avoid injury without stopping at the first sign of discomfort? Which pain signals a prelude to real injury and which pain simply requires modifying your stride? Is the self control required during a marathon focused on making your feet move when they feel like lead or slowing your feet down when they feel like they have wings? These lessons can be learned by reading and instruction but the true instructor is the marathon itself.

It's All in the Mind

This story isn't intended to be a standalone guide to marathon prep. Those can be found in the Running References section. My favorite practical reference is Humphery's "Hansons Marathon Method" and I also found useful information in "Daniels' Running Formula." As I've read books on running, I've noticed that while there is a wealth of technical information, there isn't a lot of story telling about what it feels like. I wanted to give a first person view of what it was like to stand in the start corral with thousands of other runners knowing there were 26.2 miles looming in front of me. I also wanted to provide a warning about coming out too fast and waking a certain mythological beast. The mental battle of running a marathon is more about slowing down at the beginning than it is about running through pain at the end. As running is for me, as much a mental as a physical activity, I have decided to also discuss what I was dealing with in my life, what I was thinking, and books I read before and during my training. These books helped improve my attitude not only about running but about life itself. Those can be found in the General References section.

Part 1

About Running

Benefits of Running

Meditation

For many runners, running is meditative. Some runners like to wear headphones but most do not. Some can run treadmills while others cannot stand them. I'm in the latter camps. Most of the treadmill miles I've logged have been during VO2 max testing. And headphones? I have no use for them. I prefer to hear what's going on around me. I do wear my bluetooth earpiece during most runs because I always want to be able to answer by tapping my earpiece and saying, "Sorry, I'm running a marathon right now, can you call back later?" Often I start to run with a thorny problem on my mind and by the end of the run I have thought of a solution. Music would just distract from that. Sometimes I prefer to run alone or run in silence with a group so I can think. Sometimes I prefer company and I like to talk during a run.

Talking takes away from the meditative aspect of running so more often than not I run in silence. Well that's not entirely true. I do keep my bluetooth earpiece in. I'd love to be able to answer and, be breathing easily enough to say "I'm running a marathon right now, can you give me a call in about 3 hours?" And best of all I'd love to hear the party on the other end say "I don't believe you. You don't even sound winded!"

Many runners are frustrated by repetitive courses such as repeating loops or tracks. I often prefer those courses because while they are not as boring as a treadmill, I can run them somewhat mindlessly and focus on my thoughts rather than worrying about where to turn to follow the course for the miles I need to log that day. While I like the mindlessness of running on a loop of about a mile or more, I don't like running on either ¼ mile tracks or the dreadmill. And no, that's not a typo. Those of us who love to run outdoors have a special name for the treadmill. Some people are able to listen to music, read or binge watch while running on a treadmill. I find I haven't been able to do so. Perhaps I will one day but for now I focus on running outside as being outdoors is one of the things that attracts me to running in the first place.

Digestion

Of course running burns calories. Walking also burns calories and is a lot easier on your body. The problem with walking is that while it's easier on the joints, it takes a lot longer to produce the same result. Some results you can get through running are also attainable by walking. Swimming and biking are also easier on your body but require specialized equipment and proper weather. Running can be done in a cool drizzle (ideal conditions), or a soaking rain (not fun at all), or a blizzard (fun during the first snow of the season but after that not so much), or a scorching hot day in direct sun (also not fun at all). I've run in all of these conditions and during 2015, I prayed for drizzles instead of downpours and my prayers were answered almost every time. My prayers about heat and cold were largely ignored.

The Heart

Running trains the cardiovascular system. It wakes up the heart and lungs and gets our bodies working as they were designed to work. This is the fitness benefit runners can obtain that walkers cannot aspire to. You need to get the heart rate going above a certain percentage of your maximum heart rate to properly exercise the cardiovascular system. The body makes certain adaptations during running and many of those lead to better all around health. I had a number of minor maladies that simply faded away as I started to consistently exercise. One of these was Plantar fasciitis. Others included digestive issues and high cholesterol. Walking helped with weight but it took running to control my cholesterol without medication. The Plantar fasciitis faded away once my feet and legs got stronger from so much running.

Runners' High

Another potential benefit from running is hormonal. The "runner's high" is a real thing. Once the runner reaches a certain level of exertion, the brain releases chemicals similar to those that are often sought after by addicts. The same parts of the brain are involved that are involved with alcohol, tobacco, gambling and other addictions. The difference is that with running, the "addiction" is benign, provided the runner isn't overdoing it or injuring themselves. When I was a kid, I remember thinking that athletes were doing everything with their bodies and their brains were on hold somewhere. I was wrong. The biggest battle in endurance sports is fought entirely in the mind. I was one of those "nerd" kids. I had the pocket protector, the HP RPN calculator and the only reason I didn't have the glasses pieced together with a bandage is that my eyesight was 20/20. I went out of my way to try and "prove" how unimportant physical activity was. I even had some theory that the athlete was probably daydreaming while his motor coordination was controlled by some autonomic reflexes. I scoffed at the notion that athletics could somehow make a person a better student. Now that I'm a runner, I understand that physical activity is beneficial to thought both in terms of the ability to think clearly and in terms of mood or temperament.

Love of Running

Today when I think back to the (mostly lack of) running I did over the years, only in hindsight can I perceive some of these benefits and I only wish I'd stuck with running more consistently during those middle years after I graduated from college and before I started running again in 2015. I could have had these benefits consistently in my life all along! The bottom line is that nowadays I love running! In his book, "Meb for Mortals," Meb Keflezighi said,

> "IF YOU'RE like me, you appreciate how running improves your life. You like how you feel while you're running and after a run. You like being healthier and more in control of your destiny. You like the camaraderie and the time alone. You like being outside and enjoying nature. You like pushing yourself and the satisfaction that comes from working toward a goal."

Yes, in these ways I've become a bit like Meb.

Sleep

Running helps you sleep better. Over the years, I've sometimes had difficulty sleeping. This has been particularly true in times of great stress either at work or at times of loss. Running is a natural form of exertion the body is well suited for that brings on a kind of tiredness that leads to a great night's sleep, often regardless of emotional or other stresses.

Running allows you to eat more, eat better and digest better. A sedentary lifestyle can interfere with digestion but running gets the digestive juices moving and keeps the body working at a more optimal level. I have found running gives me a good appetite as well.

Running first thing in the morning can set the tone for a peaceful, successful day. There is brain chemistry involved in running such that a hard workout can lead to an overall feeling of well being for hours afterward. This is not simply the runner's high that sometimes occurs during a run, but a lasting feeling that can make your entire day feel just right.

With all these benefits, one might come to the conclusion more is better. You can simply run your way out of your problems. This is not quite the case.

Risks and Costs of Running

Running has inherent risks. One is running too far too soon. Another is training too hard. I had a coach once explain shin splints as "too much too soon." Another risk of going too far too quickly is cardiovascular reaction. If a person with a weak heart tries to run too far, they can experience chest pain that requires medical intervention. In a worst case scenario, they can even have a heart attack. Every year people who were otherwise considered healthy drop dead from running due to cardiovascular obstructions or issues they didn't know they had.

Digestion

Running long distances risks starving internal organs of blood to send it to the legs. This means distance runners often have minor digestive issues. I mentioned better digestion as a benefit of running, but getting the bowels moving at an inopportune time is one of the slight risks of running. One thing most runners dread is a visit to the porta potty for "number two" during a race. This is a huge risk when running a long distance in another time zone. The circadian rhythm is something that does not adjust quickly and landing in a new time zone to tackle a long run without getting one's body on the new time zone first is not necessarily a good idea.

Time

Running can eat into a person's time. I know this all too well. There is time spent getting ready to run, dressing for whatever weather is happening. Then there is time spent stretching, showering and changing after the run. And believe me a runner needs to shower and change after all but the very easiest and shortest of runs. At one time I imagined that as I got used to running longer distances, my body might not sweat as much. Nope. It sweats more.

I found a TEDx talk about how running a marathon prepares a person mentally for success in business. In fact the speaker taught a college class where the final consisted of running a marathon. This is where the "cost" of running can turn into a benefit. If a runner is successful in organizing themselves in order to do enough running to start and more importantly finish an entire marathon, an important mental process has taken place. Of course finishing the marathon requires endurance but completing the marathon training requires endurance for 4 or more months. There are naysayers. There are conflicts. There are literally dozens (if not thousands!) of opportunities to "bail out" of the commitment to prepare for a marathon by running almost every single day for months on end. Successfully completing a marathon preparation program is a double-edged sword. It costs a tremendous amount of time but the reward is not only self discipline but also an accomplishment that nobody can ever deny.

The Agony of The Feet

Then there is the effect on the feet. Once you run long enough you might get broken or falling out toenails, black toenails, super thick toenails and a variety of other delightful little surprises. It is extremely important to go to a specialty running store staffed by runners and get fitted for proper running shoes. And by running store I don't mean athletic shoe or other shoe store. It needs to be a running store with a treadmill with a camera so they can film and analyze your gait. If you walk into a store and ask if they sell neutral or support running shoes and you get a blank stare, leave. Just leave.

There are two main types of running shoes. There are neutral shoes for those with high arches who strike straight. Then there are stability shoes for those with lower arches or those who tend to strike at an angle. Either their ankle is rolling in (pronation) or out (supination) and stability shoes help support the foot to prevent injuries. In my early years of running, I didn't know about any of these issues and the only pain I experienced on and off was shin splints. I got lucky because when I did run, even though I didn't have proper running shoes, I didn't go very far and I didn't run very often. If I had run frequently or run longer distances, I might have been sharing stories about early running injuries rather than happy early running experiences.

Another thing to consider in running shoes is "drop". This is the distance that the heel is higher than the toe. When I first started running, I ran in "high drop" shoes. These had drops of 10mm or more. Later, I bought some "low drop" shoes and liked running in them as well. These had drops of 6mm or less. I found that sometimes my back would be sore after running in the low drop shoes but this wasn't necessarily about the drop. A lot of the lower drop shoes also had less padding.

This is the third area to consider in running shoes. How much padding do you want? I prefer cushy shoes for long training runs and minimalist shoes for shorter training runs and races. By frequently changing shoe cushion and drop, I believe I helped prevent the kind of repetitive motion injury that might occur when running in the same shoe day in and day out.

Smart Running

The other day I was at a party at my favorite running spot. Saucony was there offering shoes we could try on for free. They contributed toward the refreshments and they provided prizes after the run. It was a big shindig and they were serving barbeque to all the runners. And by barbeque, I don't mean hot dogs and burgers cooked on a grill.

I mean ribs and pulled pork and all the fixin's. At this party, one of the coaches whose opinion I respect, Michelle came up to me and said I'm one of the smartest runners she knows. We had over 100 runners at that gathering and many of the elite 100 mile plus runners were nursing injuries. Michelle was impressed that I had improved my running without injury. My running motto is this, "No Pain, No Pain."

If something hurts I either change my stride, speed up, slow down, start walking or seek advice on how to resolve the issue. Right away. I have a chiropractor, a primary care doctor and a cardiologist and I see them annually or more often if required. I have a friend at work who ran through pain for two miles and was sidelined for six months with sore legs. No Pain. No Pain. This must be a runner's mantra whether at a 5K distance or an ultra marathon. Well, not exactly no pain. But no pain that goes beyond daily muscle soreness. Smart running can mitigate risks and allow you to recover from minor injuries before they become disabling. Smart running can mitigate risk of boredom and burnout. Smart running can allow a person to go from dabbling to running in earnest.

My Early Running

In My Youth 1960s and 70s

Elementary Through High School

When I was quite young, elementary school age, my dad used to take me to Lower Huron Metropark to run the hills. He knew I loved to run and he wanted me to learn to run fast. He would stand at the bottom and send me up each hill and I loved it. I would go to the park with other kids and they would play on the swings and slides while I ran the hills. Recently my cousin and I talked and he related a story to me about a time when I ran off and left him in the dust, just keeping him in sight and speeding up every time he started to close the distance. Yes I loved to run and it came naturally to me. But for some reason I never took competitive running seriously.

I was a cross country runner in high school. For one season. We weren't poor, but we were working class and I couldn't afford cross country spikes. The coach at U of D High let me use some moldy old spikes that were laying around. I only ran one 5K meet and fell at about mile 2 and got a rock through my knee. I had other athletes call out to me "Don't look down" so of course I looked down and saw blood streaming from my knee. I finished the race but I was sidelined for the rest of the season. It wasn't really that painful. I went to urgent care or whatever it was called back then and got it bandaged up but I didn't even go to cross country practices after that race. One run in one season, circa 1973. That was my cross country career in high school. No varsity letters for me!

The Army

My college attendance was on again off again. I started and stopped college more than a few times. At one point, I decided I was ready to make a real go of finishing college so I joined the Army and applied for West Point at the same time. At the time, I was living in San Francisco. I went down to the local recruiting station and took the ASVAB (vocational aptitude battery) test. I scored high and the job they had available was "93 Juliette, Air Traffic Control Radar" so I took it.

As an adopted person, I've always been frustrated with the hoops I had to jump through every time I wanted to prove my identity. I couldn't just wander down to City Hall in Detroit and ask for a birth certificate. Oh no. Mine had to come from the state capitol in Lansing, Michigan and it always took eight weeks. So when I was a continent away from where I was born, I expected it to take weeks for them to figure out who I was. Nope. It took 5 minutes and they knew my birth name in 5 minutes. In 1976, before the internet they knew facts about me that it would take any civilian authority 8 weeks to learn. I never forgot the contrast in how long it takes to get an answer, depending on who is asking for data.

In the Army, my favorite PT (Physical Training) was running. I could run circles around the rest of the company. I also enjoyed the "inverted crawl" which was a sort of running around on all fours only you were doing it in something that resembles the "bridge" position in Yoga. There was also a peculiar sort of punishment the drill sergeant had worked out that involved "sitting on the wall." The recruit would "sit" unsupported with their back against a wall and after only a few seconds of this, most men would limp away giving the appearance of having just had a severe beating. I was asked to do this one time and I stood up and walked calmly away. I figured out I needed to "ham it up" for the rest of the platoon in order to avoid having him come up with something else that might have been more effective. After boot camp and advanced training, I was assigned to the the 82D Airborne at Fort Bragg, NC. I guess it was considered poetic justice since I grew up in Detroit and the 82D had been brought in to quell the Detroit riots 10 years earlier.

In the military, we did daily PT. It seemed like nothing to me at the time. We did jumping jacks, pushups and running. I snickered about how easy it was. My company commander let me train with the 82D Airborne Pathfinders as a prep for West Point. The Pathfinders are a little-known group of special ops types who parachute in ahead of the main group and their PT is extreme compared to what normal troops do. The Green Berets also trained at Fort Bragg, NC but I never got a chance to train with them. To me the stuff the Pathfinders were doing was quite enough. My favorite of the Pathfinder exercises were the "buddy runs" where we ran 100 yards or so with another guy on our back. When I was officially admitted to West Point, I begged off of jump school because an injury at jump school might have meant missing the chance of a lifetime to attend West Point.

West Point

It turns out I also ran in college. Once. At West Point, they give admission preference to high school athletes so I made sure I put on my application that I ran Cross Country in high school even if it was only one meet in one season 😀. There is a custom for "plebes" (fourth classmen / freshmen) to eat "Square" meals at West Point. I was already underweight and I actually could wear a shirt with a neck size of 13! Square meals involved staring straight ahead and making exaggerated square movements to get each and every fork full of food into one's mouth. It turns out the guys on varsity sports got to skip that square meal nonsense. I knew I would starve if I kept eating "Square" meals so I decided to go out as a walk on for the sport I was best at: Cross Country. At the time I didn't know the distance was double the 5K we ran in high school CC! I wasn't into photos back then but my aunt Juanita snapped a photo of my cousins David and Larry and I while I was home for Christmas.

I ran cross country for West Point against Rutgers. In one meet. I slowed down as I approached the 10K finish line and let some Rutgers guy pass me. I could see the coach scowling at me as I passed. Then he cut me and everyone after me. I seem to remember seeing a time on the clock of 31:54 for 6.2 miles which is pretty close to 5 minutes a mile. I went back and looked at NCAA results for the season I ran in 1977. With a time like that I could have gone to NCAA finals in Spokane, Washington that year, so I'm pretty sure my time was slower, perhaps around 36 minutes. At the time I wondered if he decided to make my time the cut point to set an example not to slow down at the end. I'll never know for sure but one message I got was, "Don't slow down until *after* crossing the finish line!"

Once I was cut, I decided to quit running because the practices were so tiring. We used to run what seemed at the time to be a thousand miles a day. Then the elite athletes would add on more miles by running on the governor's estate rather than returning to campus. I never opted for "extra" miles and I wonder if my experience would have been better if I had done so. This was another lesson I took away from my "one meet in one season" college cross-country experience, that working harder could lead to success. Though I was cut, as the fastest of the cut athletes I was allowed to stay with the team as "manager". This meant I could continue to sit at "Corps Squad" tables and eat normal meals. We beat Navy in football that year so everybody got to stop eating square meals after that great victory. I had been eating "normal" since the start of cross country season and I was feeling healthier because of it. In the second semester of my plebe year, I decided to leave West Point. I often regret not staying longer and I wonder if I might have gone out for track or cross country again if I had stayed.

A Long Holiday from Running

Early Career

After the Army, I returned to Michigan to finish my engineering degree at U of D and during that time I didn't think of running one little bit. I got busy with classes and physically tended to let myself go. I learned to embrace my inner couch potato. The most strenuous activities I did were downhill skiing and cross country skiing and both of those not very often. And I did quite a few twelve ounce curls. I enjoyed the feeling I got with physical exertion but I forgot about how good I would feel after a longer distance run.

After finishing college, early in my engineering career I ran again once with my cousin David when he was living in Minnesota. I turned about 7 shades of red running on a hot, humid afternoon with him. He was worried for me and suggested we walk the rest of the way. This experience seemed to confirm my decision not to run. I went back to the couch and mostly stayed there. I was a skinny kid. I had always been skinny. I remember trying to do stuff to gain weight. One of my favorite things was to go down to the cafeteria at work and order a banana split. I would get one almost every day! The others were jealous because they couldn't even look at a thing like that without gaining pounds. I had a 29 inch waist and weighed in the 130s. One reason for the banana split was to gain weight. Another was to give myself some form of reward for working in a windowless office. I had a windowless office when I worked for the Air Force in Rome, NY. I again had a windowless office at Chrysler. Somehow two of the earliest jobs in my engineering career came with "cave-like" office spaces.

Family

I met my wife Michele in 1987 and on one of our early dates, she prepared dinner for me at her house. It was wonderous. She had made me two fried chickens and a huge pan of spaghetti. I almost proposed to her on the spot! I did propose a few months later and when we got married, the pounds came promptly. Michele was a great cook and she made me a special project. My weight shot up to "normal" and my waist size got up as far as 38 before I started thinking it might be time for it to come back the other way.

We had two kids. Our son, Chris was a premie born in 1991. Our van was broken into while I was in the delivery room with my wife. I had parked on the street outside Hutzel Hospital and when I came outside after Chris was born I found the drivers' side window smashed. I don't even remember what they took only that I didn't really care that much because I was a new father! Chris got out of intensive care before Michele did. While he got out of ICU, we weren't allowed to bring him home until he weighed 5 pounds. This took some time. We took him to our last Lamaze class. It was pretty funny. The rest of the class were still weeks away from their deliveries and we were already done.

Our daughter, Liz was born in 1995. She came on time and we were able to relax in a nice birthing suite at a local hospital where our car was left untouched. This was a much better experience for all of us and Michele and Liz were able to come home from the hospital together. As I watched my kids grow up, I was impressed by how much they loved running and the outdoors in general. As I didn't grow up with siblings, I also watched my kids to learn more about myself.

My son played baseball and I was one of the volunteer coaches. Our team won the city league several times. My son was involved with Boy Scouts from first grade right through high school and I was a volunteer adult leader through all that time. I went to almost every meeting, field trip and camp out. I had gone backpack camping once in college in upstate New York and I'd loved it so I almost never missed a chance to go on a camp out with my son, even though most scout camp outs were car-camping at local Boy Scout camps or state parks. I loved the outdoors and this was probably reinforced by the experience I'd had working in windowless offices early in my career. I always looked forward to getting outside. I loved the sky and the smell of the outdoors, especially the woods. Chris loved going on the ski trips with the Boy Scouts. One time he was showing off to a girl in the terrain park and wound up having to pay a visit to Northern Michigan Hospital.

My daughter played basketball in middle school and high school and one of my favorite pictures is a photo another parent took of her going up for a basket. Liz was jumping so high in the air all the defenders were at or below her shoulders! She had to give up basketball as a high school freshwoman when she was sidelined with a foot injury. In fact, she was sidelined several years in a row and most of the pictures I have of her during her high school years, she was wearing a cast. Perhaps watching my kids battle injuries helped me to settle down when I took up running so I wouldn't earn "frequent flyer" status at the local urgent care.

During these middle decades when I was not running, my needs to be outdoors were largely met by being at scout camp with my son. When we weren't going to one of our kids' athletic events or music recitals, my wife and I were almost always doing stuff like going to the symphony or live theater. Michele and I were an excellent match for one another and we were deeply in love and deeply interested in one another. She was a pharmacist and I an engineer and we were mutually interested in and curious about one another's professions. We enjoyed hours of conversation about technical topics. She could go on for hours about pharmacology, subtle differences between drug names and kinetic dosing as I could go on about physics and circuit theory. There was never a time we weren't fascinated with one another intellectually and physically. With this great relationship with my wife and raising two very active children together, there simply was no time for daily or even weekly running around our house.

Michele and I did manage to get outdoors riding horseback, walking and skiing together but not very often. I never convinced her to go on to camp with Chris but she did make it to Girl Scout with Liz once or twice. Michele wasn't as interested in the outdoors as I was. She got her outdoor fix tending the plantings in our garden and for many years I never even knew what a weed looked like.

Susan B Komen Race for the Cure April 2008

In late 2007 my wife was diagnosed with Breast Cancer. My son and I were already in training for a 14 day hike at Philmont Scout Ranch in New Mexico coming up in Summer 2008 so adding a 5K run to raise money for Cancer research seemed like a "no-brainer". I was off the couch that year but only to train for 14 days hiking from 7,000 to 12,500 feet with a 50 pound pack.

As the first organized race I'd run since college, I was impressed with the crowd support, bands playing along the course and the sheer number of runners. It was fun. It was perhaps at Komen 2008 that a seed got planted in my mind that I would run again someday. The weather was nice. This is incredibly important for somebody new to running or coming back after a long absence. Good weather makes for a positive all around experience. It was not too hot or too cold and there was no rain to deal with either.

The run started at Comerica Park and proceeded north on Woodward away from downtown for about a mile and a half. I could see the faster runners already coming back as I headed north. When I saw those fast runners coming back, I felt jealous and wished I was faster but I knew I couldn't get great or even good at something by merely wishing so I enjoyed my run for what it was: a day out with my kids raising money to fight breast cancer.

Once we made a loop at the north end near Wayne State, we proceeded south on Woodward toward Comerica Park. We ran around the park and finished on the south side. I ran 28 minutes and change in the Komen 5K which seemed fast to me at the time but my kids were both waiting impatiently for me at the end.

My wife's cancer treatment was uneventful and she would be in complete remission by the end of the summer. I was unhappy with my 28-ish minute performance in the Komen 5K but I threw it out of my mind and went back to preparing for my upcoming Philmont hike.

Philmont Summer 2008

Preparation

I went with my son Chris to Philmont in July 2008. Philmont is the Disney World of scouting and troops are often on multi-year waiting lists to get a slot. A Philmont trek is a lot like a multi-day marathon. We pick up provisions about every 3 days and divide up the freeze dried food among the 10 crew members. Hauling water back to camp and purifying it were daily chores tackled by the younger scouts. Younger, fitter, faster crew members also take more weight during the hikes.

I joined the local gym and hired a personal trainer to get me ready. He had me running 30 flights of stairs a day with a pack. He had me doing a lot of walking and a bit of running. Our crew did a lot of practice hikes with pack but I had missed some of them taking Michele to some of her treatments. Still at the time I thought I was in the best shape of my life.

Getting to New Mexico

Our crew flew down together. I tried taking a nice lighter along but TSA now owns it. Darn. We took a bus from Denver to Colorado Springs to spend a day that included local tourist attractions including the US Air Force Academy. This was my second visit to USAFA and it reminded me of my visit there for a football game in 1977. When I was at West Point, I got randomly selected to fly there to see the Army Air Force football game. We flew there on military transport planes sitting on webbing like paratroopers and ate box lunches in flight.

Army won. Of course. In the 70's, before Colorado Springs was built up much, I had been impressed by how USAFA looked like a settlement built on another planet. On this visit, there were still a few vantage points from which you could imagine

USAFA was a self contained facility constructed on a moon of some distant planet. After USAFA, we visited a Colorado Springs attraction called Seven Falls. We then had dinner at the Flying W ranch, and we got a night's sleep before boarding the bus to go on to New Mexico and prepare for our Philmont hike. The stop in Colorado Springs was designed to allow our bodies a chance to start adjusting to the altitude. There were enough stairs to climb at Seven Falls we could begin to come to grips with the way our bodies might handle exertion at altitude.

Chris and I had already spent a lot of weekends together as he was growing up as I went on almost every cub scout and boy scout camp out during those years. When his turn came to go to Philmont, of course I wanted to go! We had already signed up and paid when Michele got her cancer diagnosis so I wound up dividing my time between Philmont practice hikes and taking Michele to chemo and other activities as well. This lack of focus on Philmont preparation resulted in me being less prepared than I would like to have been. Being relatively unprepared, along with randomly tacking on extra miles to what was already an 80+ mile hike was a little more than I bargained for. There was some discussion among the adults of our crew about my physical conditioning while we hiked Philmont, especially on the longer days. I would say Philmont was my first experience with "Bonking". My experience at Philmont was an important lesson for me that being prepared is important if you want to enjoy rather than suffer from physical exertion.

Base Camp

In Cimarron New Mexico, the Philmont Boy Scout camp has an area near the road where hundreds of tents are set up. There are a handful of large fire pits and these are the only areas where fires are allowed during drought conditions. We were there during drought conditions. Each crew signs out gear for the upcoming hike that includes large pots to boil and purify water, rope to hang the bear bags and other essentials. There are wild animals at Philmont including bears and mountain lions. You don't want anything smelling like food in your tent with you so we had to put all our food into a mesh bag and hang it 25 feet off the ground in "bear bags". One of the activities in base camp was instruction on how to use bear bags as well as how to use the "sump". The sump is a small pit where we drained food scraps so the smell wouldn't attract large predators, mainly bears. We also got to meet our ranger that day. She was the person who would go with us the first few days to make sure we were getting things right, including water purification, cooking and safe food scrap disposal.

There was a large rally the night before our hike but I opted to skip it and stayed in my tent. I felt it was better to get more sleep so I went to bed early. I could hear it getting started but I think I made the right choice to be well rested going into an 85+ mile hike through the mountains. The day we set out, they put us on an old rusty school bus with no windows and drove us quite a distance up into the mountains above base camp. I remember thinking, "We have to walk all the way back, don't we?"

Stairmaster

Our first few days hiking took us through the northern half of Philmont. There is a particularly difficult climb called "Stairmaster" that takes us up to a camp site called "Ponil." Ponil was base camp many years ago but now it was just one of several staffed camps we would visit. Our crew leader

August opted to skip Stairmaster by taking us by a much longer but less steep route. The route was not as steep but meant walking about double the distance of Stairmaster. We got to Ponil exhausted from walking so far but in talking to other crews I think we missed out on a particularly unpleasant section by going August's way. Still, tacking on extra miles was one of the factors that contributed to my feeling of exhaustion as the days wore on.

Both High and Low on the Same Day

A few days later we found ourselves atop Baldy, the highest point for dozens if not hundreds of miles. It was breathtaking and I'm so glad we opted to include this in our hike even if reaching the summit was difficult. The scouts took turns leading each day's hike. One dad had a GPS unit we could consult if we got badly lost and we had large maps with latitude and longitude grids we could use to figure out where we were if necessary. On the way down from Baldy, the scout leading our group missed a turn and we wound up "bushwacking." Bushwacking is a term which means hiking through the woods where there is no trail. It can take about triple the effort of following a marked trail. The rule is that as soon as you realize you are off the trail, you are supposed to double back, find the trail and resume hiking. For some reason, it took us some time to figure out we were lost and rather than find our way back, we opted for a "short cut" to rejoin the trail up ahead.

This was not a good idea. It was beginning to get dark by the time we finally found our way back to our intended trail and we barely made it back in time to make dinner, get to bed and rest for the next day's hike which was to be the longest hike of our entire trip. When you're doing something difficult, inadequate rest is never a good thing. So we had been both high and low on the same day. We had the experience of being on a mountaintop followed only a few hours later by the experience of being lost and barely making it back to camp before dark.

Enough!

Bonking is a phenomenon where the body says "enough" during an intense physical activity. More often than not it's all in the mind. Sometimes the mind calculates you shouldn't be doing this and somehow the muscles fall into line with the thought process and provide "evidence" you shouldn't be doing this and before you know it you're walking instead of running. Sometimes the muscles start a revolt and you get increasing soreness or fatigue. At Philmont, on the day of the longest hike, we went down about 1,000 slippery feet, then had to climb almost as far in the afternoon. I already have trouble with heights so I was wiped out before we even made it to the climb. Cumulative fatigue had taken effect. I hadn't put my water bladder together correctly so water was leaking down my back instead or providing me essential hydration during the afternoon uphill portion of the hike.

By afternoon, other members of the crew were helping with my pack and I was considering taking a day off and riding to the next checkpoint by jeep! This is what Bonking is all about. The body is sending a loud and clear "I QUIT" signal to the brain and depending on how bad things really are, you have no choice but to listen. In the embedded software world, this is called a "non-maskable interrupt." It's like somebody hitting the reset button on a computer, it has no choice but to reboot. Bonking is the non-maskable interrupt of the athlete. Whatever agenda had been planned is no longer relevant, the new agenda involves allowing the body to recover.

Interestingly enough, the hike up from base camp at 9,000 feet to the 12,500 foot summit of "Baldy" a day earlier had been more difficult but the awesome splendor of being on the tallest point for hundreds of miles had been enough of a psychological boost to distract from cumulative fatigue. That day Chris had volunteered to carry my stuff up to the summit for me. That helped as well. The power of the mind to overcome fatigue was an important lesson for me that I would later draw upon during long distance runs.

Good Pain vs Bad Pain

At this point, I'd like to revisit the topic of pain. At Philmont, we had a lot of pain. We had shoulder pain from the straps of the heavy packs. We had leg pain from all the hiking. We had back pain. We had foot pain from all the walking in heavy hiking boots. I did not have any blisters. None. I really splurged on Philmont when it came to equipment. I bought proper hiking boots and proper socks. I had learned this lesson in the Army. The Army didn't splurge on us but they made sure we had excellent boots! I also made sure I purchased proper clothing that was lightweight and versatile. We had conditions ranging from chilly at night to quite hot in the direct sun during the day. We had weather ranging from bright sun to gentle rain and we even had one day when three inches of hail fell on us during a thunderstorm. Earlier, when I mentioned the risks and costs of running, I said my motto was "No Pain, No Pain" and I promised to come back to the topic of pain.

Pain can be a good thing. It means your body is working properly and all your nerve endings are sending proper signals. If you go for a long walk when you're not accustomed to walking and have sore feet that evening but feel fine in the morning, that fits my definition of "no pain." This is what Philmont was like for me. I wasn't in the shape I would have liked to have been in so I had some rough days but I never had a nagging pain that carried on day in and day out. All it took for me to feel better was a good night's rest.

If you're walking, running, jogging, lifting weights, skydiving or swimming and you have nagging pain day in and day out, consult a professional. There are massage therapists that can find and release muscle groups that have become knotted. There are coaches and exercise physiologists that can prescribe treatment or exercises based on symptoms. There are chiropractors and there are doctors that can recognize areas of concern and provide advice or even treatment when necessary. Never walk around with nagging or chronic pain thinking "this is normal." Endurance athletes are not heroes. Nobody would be doing this stuff if it hurt all the time.

Remember my mantra: No pain. No pain. If I had chronic pain that day at Philmont when I felt like I couldn't go any further, I would have made them bring that jeep and take me down to base camp to recover. What I did have was fatigue and after a night's rest I was able to finish the rest of the hike. I define good pain as muscle soreness that takes less than a day or two to go away with rest and recovery. Mild pain or soreness is a constant companion to a person who is exercising and pushing their limits but it needs to be something they can be comfortable with. This is a tricky area for runners. We get used to running long distances and putting up with pain so we need to really have a laser focus on intensity, sharpness, and duration of any pain.

Soreness that comes from exertion can feel good. It makes me feel alive. No more couch potato here! While all my outdoor experiences with my son's boy scout troop helped prepare me to accept and embrace routine soreness as a welcome thing, Philmont got me to the level where I was dealing with discomfort day in day out for more than a week. I loved it and not because I like being sore. I thought it was worth it to be surrounded by all that natural beauty and enjoy the excellent companionship of my son and the other members of our Philmont crew.

Junior Olympics Summer 2012

Maxed Out

In 2012, as a high school senior, my daughter Liz joined a Detroit area running team called Maximum Output Track Club (Maxed Out). While she had played basketball in middle school and high school, and ran track in high school, she had not played a sport outside of school until now. Maxed Out is a very competitive Detroit area track club that attracts some of the better local athletes and they take about a dozen of them to Junior Olympics every year.

During school, Liz had gone to Oakland County finals almost every year and she was the fifth fastest 100m sprinter in the county in her age group. I was so proud of her with every track medal she brought home. She kept placing well in meets and I remember her Maxed Out coach saying he wasn't sure Liz would make Junior Olympics because he wasn't sure she was taking her running seriously enough. I snickered because I knew Liz could do whatever she put her mind to. I was right.

Liz was running better and better. She never missed a practice and often came in first at meets. When she qualified for Junior Olympics in Houston, our coach had to eat a little crow. I cashed in miles and bought us tickets right away. She wanted to be in a room with her teammates so I took a room by myself. Michele couldn't adjust her work schedule to come with us so it was me and Liz for a very hot week in Houston. And let me assure you. It. Was. HOT.

Houston Heat

I began to understand what we were up against when we arrived at our hotel and when I was making trips to my car to bring stuff in, my glasses would fog instantly as I passed the first set of doors leaving the lobby to go outside. The humidity was that high. By the time the second set of doors opened, I thought somebody had tossed me in an oven set to "BROIL." I remember driving around Houston, seeing people outdoors doing things like having picnics and playing softball and thinking to myself, "Are they crazy? Don't they know how HOT it is?" It was in these conditions we went to the track for Liz to compete.

In Texas, they take their high school football very seriously. This high school had stands bigger than those I'd seen for a lot of college teams and they had a jumbotron. A color jumbotron at a high school football stadium? Well this was Texas! And make no mistake, this thing was a stadium, not a mere field. Liz's event required her to run 100m the first day to make the cut to go to semi finals.

She ran the 100m in 13.4 seconds but didn't advance. The winner of that heat ran 11.99 seconds. I was proud of her for just making it to Junior Olympics in the first place.

In this heat it didn't bother me one bit that the times she ran in Humble, TX were slower than her previous PR for the 100m. Even for a sprinter, heat can be a very bad thing. At the time, I still had no direct interest in running, especially in all that heat! But just as I had watched my kids when they were younger for insight into myself, there was a seed growing in my mind that my daughter was good at running and she might have gotten some of that from me.

Health

Healthy Body

Beginning in the mid 1980s, I spent the first 17 years of my engineering career at Chrysler and over the years they harped and harped on developing healthy habits and maintaining healthy weight. They did this because it saved them money. Healthy employees had fewer health care claims. I would go to the occasional meetings they held on healthy cooking and healthy eating but for the most part I embraced the comfortable lifestyle I enjoyed that mostly involved sitting at a desk all day and sitting on the couch at home after a full, satisfying meal. My wife's efforts to transform me from a "skinny kid" to an average man had been entirely successful and at first I didn't see a reason to mess with that success.

Later, in the mid 2000's I took a job at GM and they harped on many the same healthy habits. The car companies were all starting to connect the dots that unhealthy lifestyle and overweight led to higher insurance costs. Larger companies often "self insure" which means they have billions of dollars set aside in their budgets for employee health claims and they pay "insurers" strictly to administer claims. They don't really pay premiums. This means that if these companies could figure out how to get the average employee thinking about healthy diet, lifestyle and weight, there were millions of dollars in savings in it for them. GM offered financial incentives for getting annual checkups and attending cooking or other classes on healthy lifestyle. These financial incentives were part of what finally got me motivated to get to a healthier weight.

I started gradually adopting healthier habits. This was not easy because my wife was a cooking savant. She could taste something once or twice then go out on the internet, find the recipe, tweak it and we'd be eating the same meal at home. She loved to cook ribs. Greasy ribs. Fried chicken. Oh GOD how I loved her fried chicken! So in 2012, when I decided to lose weight in earnest, I took a 2 pronged approach. I wanted to get down from 203+ pounds to the upper middle of a "healthy BMI" for my height. I wanted to lose about 40 pounds. I started ordering mostly salads at restaurants and I started walking about 6 miles a day. At my job, it was easy to pile on walking miles as GM's Warren Tech Center campus is over a square mile of scattered buildings fairly well connected by sidewalks and little traffic.

By fall of 2013 my approach had partially worked. I had lost about 25 pounds and my waist was back to a bit more healthy 36, but that last 15 pounds refused to budge. It was then that GM brought in someone who offered a weight loss challenge with a cash prize for the person who lost the highest percentage of their body weight. The instructor offered Herbalife shakes for weight loss but I was already using Shaklee vitamins so I opted for the Shaklee 180 meal replacement protein shakes. I signed up and started using the calorie counting app Myfitnesspal. I got my stubborn 15 pounds off and reached the low 160's before thanksgiving 2013. And I kept it off. The instructor became gravely ill and the class unraveled and though I probably would have won the cash prize, I won the real prize which was that I was living at my healthy weight of about 160 pounds!

Healthy Mind

At the same time I was getting to a healthy weight, I also increased my reading. I did a lot of reading. I picked up several sci fi series and read them as ebooks. Over the years our family had read the Harry Potter books together as they came out. I remember one night when people were standing in line at the local Borders to pick up their copies, the local grocery store had them in stock so we grabbed two copies there. Even though we could often finish a Harry Potter book in less than a day, the four of us didn't want to wait for the others to finish so we almost never bought less than two copies. But my reading began to increase dramatically. Michele and I used to binge watch episodes of Sherlock Holmes or Perry Mason but when I started reading more, we would often be sitting together reading rather than binge watching.

I enjoyed The Giver series, Pandemonium series, Legend series, Hunger Games series, Enders Game series and the Divergent series. In the Divergent series, at one point a main character I felt a strong connection to died and I felt genuine heartache. I visited online forums and participated discussions about Veronica Roth's decision to employ this particular plot twist. I picked up The Giver series after having enjoyed Number the Stars and I was rewarded with an excellent set of stories with well developed characters. One thing many of these dystopian series had in common was ordinary heroes who had to persevere through difficult circumstances. I remember the tiredness I would feel as I trudged through difficult chapters. I think this helped mentally prepare me for endurance sports as I came to appreciate perseverance as a quality I aspired to have myself.

I enjoyed The Book Thief and I was inspired by the character Rudy Steiner who loved to run and admired Jesse Owens. This was the thing the Nazis feared the most, that people under their occupation could come to admire someone of "inferior race." I was touched by the characters in the book, Hans and Rosa Hubermann who adopted Liesel Meminger. I could relate to Liesel as I was beginning to pick up reading more. I also read the Fault in Our Stars. I found it uplifting despite its serious subject. I could relate to the story but I couldn't imagine it might be preparing me for things to come.

Shaklee

During the weight loss challenge I was drinking Shaklee 180 shakes and taking Vita Lea multivitamins. I hadn't felt so alive in years! I tried to convince Michele to join me on my longer walks but alas, she was having joint trouble. She had total knee replacement in November 2013, right about the time I hit my weight goal and she was unable to so much as join me on one of my walks. Michele and I did manage to make it to LA Fitness for water aerobics. We loved those classes and hardly missed until her surgery. After her surgery, we never quite figured out how to get back to walking or to those water aerobics classes again. This was another strong lesson for me: injuries can totally disrupt lifestyle so avoid them at all cost!

From 2012 to 2014 I was walking about 6 miles a day according to the step counter on my iPhone. So when I say zero or couch to Boston, I'm not being entirely honest. I started from walking roughly 6 miles a day which is not really the same as running but is not exactly the couch either. The feeling of youth, vitality, strength and well being I had after beginning the Shaklee vitamin regimen definitely contributed to my decision to take up running again.

Shaklee vitamins are sold through a multi level marketing organization and they are not cheap. They have a web site you can go through to order them but ultimately the sale is "credited" to the person in their multilevel marketing organization through whom you set up your Shaklee account. There is a lot of literature and anecdotal evidence about the benefits of "real" vitamins for health but not a lot of mainstream research. The reason big pharma doesn't do research on this topic is they can't patent vitamins.

About this time, the FDA published a report saying that over the counter vitamins were essentially worthless because there was no enforcement of what they contained. Yes you read that right. You can go down and buy some vitamins at the local store that claim to contain vitamin C and there is no actual enforcement to make sure what is on the label reflects what is in the vitamins you just bought. Meanwhile Shaklee publishes peer-reviewed research not only that their vitamins contain what is claimed on the label but the absorption rate is well understood and documented. In short, I'd rather have 100 mg of Shaklee vitamin C than 10,000 mg of somebody's store brand.

Turning Point

Wedding Vows Renewed

In Spring of 2014, Michele and I went on our second honeymoon to celebrate 25 years of marriage. It was a wonderful trip! I was delighted to find that Royal Caribbean had eliminated that eating binge known as the midnight buffet and was offering smaller portions at meals. You could always order more but by default the portions were sensible. We came back from our trip pretty much weighing the same as we did when we left. I was so happy we could go indulge for a week and come back without feeling like we'd been "fattened up".

During our trip, we'd arranged to have our wedding vows renewed at the cathedral in Nassau Bahamas. It was a simple private exchange of vows with just Michele and I and the monsignor. We had everything scripted with parts for all three of us to say where Michele and I promised one another a lifetime of love. We never suspected we had any less time to look forward to than the quarter century we had already enjoyed together.

Cancer

Not long after that trip my wife got deathly ill. Michele called me just before the July 4th weekend in 2014 to say she wouldn't be coming home from work and that instead she was going to the ER! The ER?!? What?!? The next day they did a biopsy to determine what was causing the pain in her right breast and about a week later we got the official result.

Michele had stage 4 breast cancer that was in her right breast and left lymph nodes. They didn't do a very good job explaining the prognosis to us and both Michele and I assumed it would be like it was when she had breast cancer the first time. It was not. This time Michele had triple negative metastatic breast cancer. For the next 90 days I became her primary caregiver. I lost even more weight and my doctor warned me I had gone too far. My goal had been 160 but now I was passing 140 heading for 130. Being a caregiver for a person who is terminally ill is all-consuming. I did not take care of myself and I did not take care of business. Things around the house broke and didn't get fixed. Decisions lingered without being made. I ignored important letters and bills. It's a good thing I had put most things on automatic bill pay or we'd probably have started having shut off notices. At first the struggles involved getting her to eat during chemo and getting her to an ever increasing array of appointments and treatments. Then they escalated to include 24 hour a day pain management.

The Flood of 2014

In August 2014 there was a torrential rainstorm that caused a flood that was unlike anything seen in hundreds of years. At my job, half the facility was under 3 feet of water. I planned to work from home but I was asked by management to come in for the meeting. That was the last straw. With the network down, phone lines down and half the complex flooded, I did my best to lead a meeting with dozens of attendees scattered around a dozen time zones.   After that meeting I went to the restroom and the proceeded to forget the way to the elevator. This kind of temporary memory loss was a red flag so I talked to my doctor about what had happened and at his suggestion, I didn't go back to work. I took leave from work and I focused on taking care of my wife.

Chemo

I remember particularly poignant situation during Michele's illness. For chemo, Michele would need a port. The chemicals they use for chemo are extremely toxic. The nurse administering the treatment must wear protective clothing. Chemo is poison. It is targeted poison but it is poison nonetheless. The reason they want to install a port is so that the chemo can go directly into the bloodstream close to the heart and reach the target cells quickly. When given through an IV, the veins can become damaged by the chemo. We went to a special outpatient area of the hospital where they do ports and picc lines and waited. The room was different than most. The ceiling light lenses weren't clear. They were made of photographs of sky or flowers or nature scenes. I guess they thought this was calming for people going through these often tedious procedures.

The procedure was relatively uneventful and we went home, expecting everything to go as smoothly as it had when Michele had a port installed for her previous round of chemo in 2008. A few days later the skin around the port ruptured and a small amount of fluid started coming out. It turns out the cancer had spread so much it was impossible to do a port.

They took the port back out and Michele started getting her chemo via IV. The chemo didn't work at all. Michele got very sick and was too sick to travel. We wanted to visit the Block Center in Chicago where they offered more integrated cancer treatment that involved a vegan diet and the very latest techniques. We managed to make it there once but Michele was too sick to ever go back.

Reality Check

At the beginning, Michele swore me to secrecy. She didn't want friends and family knowing she was sick. This means I was unable to reach out for support. By late summer, after that failed port, I had had enough and let everyone know. I planned a surprise birthday party for Michele. The idea was that everyone would get a chance to come visit with her. She got wind of the plan and put the kibosh on the party. When we went to see her surgeon for routine follow-up, I remember the eerily prophetic thing she told us. When Michele explained she would rather not have people over for her birthday and would rather have them come at Thanksgiving, the surgeon who is a close friend said in response, "How do you know you will be alive then?" This may have seemed like somewhat a rude thing to say but we had been carrying on like this cancer was trivial. It was not trivial and I'm thankful for that reality check.

Grief

By September, I had a stair lift put in the house. I didn't want Michele to have to move to the dining room like so many people do when they start having problems with stairs. The dining room was the most important room in the house to her and Thanksgiving was Michele's high feast day. I knew she would rather sit on the thing and ride up than have the dining room gutted so she could have a hospital bed on the first floor. By the time it was installed, Michele was only able to use it for 2 weeks before she became too weak and disoriented to use it. I called to have it removed and in the few weeks it took to get through to the company, Michele grew even sicker.

One day we called EMS to the house because Michele was too disoriented to ride in my car to the ER and when they checked her oxygen they refused to take her to the hospital of our choice. By law, when a person's oxygen is as low as Michele's they must proceed directly to the closest ER. It was at this closest hospital Michele declined even more rapidly. She had fluid on her lungs. I sat with her in the ICU and calmed her to keep her from squirming while they performed a procedure called thoracentesis (removing fluid from the lungs). She grew stronger for a few days and we asked them to move her to palliative care so she could be more comfortable.

The last thing Michele had searched for on her iPhone was "side effects of morphine." She was strongly against taking morphine and preferred her pain management be done with different meds. In palliative care, they insisted on a cocktail that included an opiate and Ativan. I was against the use of Ativan because it made her so drowsy, she couldn't function. Michele had lost the ability to speak and mostly babbled in baby talk. When her best friend Wanda came to see her, Michele became lucid and spoke clearly for a few hours while Wanda was there. This would be the last conversation any of us would have with Michele. She died a few days later on October 10, 2014. Her funeral was October 18, 2014.

After Michele passed I drifted for a time. I kept eating the healthy things I was eating before and she wasn't there to cook me the unhealthy things I loved (and missed). I gained some weight back but not very much. Going from a family of four to an empty nester, to a widower left me with a lot of time on my hands. I wanted some kind of outlet that wasn't unhealthy but I really never considered running until my brother in law suggested it out of the blue. Well it was out of the Maize and Blue...

Part 2

Running Again

Running for Fun

Trail to the Victors Spring 2015

In March of 2015, my brother in law invited me to run in the Trail to the Victors (Big House 5K) race at UofM in early April. It was sponsored by Toyota and I work at GM so I thought it might be awkward but I decided to sign up anyway. My son lived a few blocks from the Big House so I was over there all the time anyway. I signed up and paid for the race. I was hoping to reconnect with family as we were drifting apart. Michele had been the glue that held our family together and I was willing to try anything to spend more time with family.

The BH5K bib pickup was at Crisler Arena in Ann Arbor. It wasn't enough to drive to Ann Arbor once, we had to go twice. Once to pick up our bibs and another time to run in the race. When i got there, they wanted me to know my bib number.

Bib number? Are you kidding? I know my name. Why can't I just use that? So I looked up my bib number online. And no, not on my smartphone. There's no LTE or even 3G anywhere near bib pickup. Luckily they had computers you could walk up to and look up your bib number by name. I later learned these kiosks are a standard feature at larger runs. I got my bib and headed home to rest up for the race. I was unsure how I'd do because I hadn't run since Komen in 2008.

The day of the 5K came. This was my first 5K in almost six years! My previous 5K was the Komen race for the cure in 2008. Before Komen, I hadn't run in a timed race in over 30 years. The crowd at the BH5K was impressive. The starting corrals stretched for blocks and blocks. I didn't care where I started. I just wanted to run so I found a spot where I could hear everything and settled in to wait for the start. I lost track of other family members who were there for the same race in that huge crowd. Our bibs had "chips" on them so when we passed over mats at the start and finish lines, our times could be recorded.

At the start of the race it was cool but comfortable. No icy winds. No rain. No snow. No scorching heat. It was what I would later call "perfect" running weather. I just enjoyed it and didn't really understand all the nuances. The beginning of the race went up an incline. To me it was no sweat. This took me back to my childhood days when my dad had me run up hills at Lower Huron Metropark. He used to love watching me run up those hills and encouraged me to do it all the time. I learned to love running hills from an early age. So here I was at the start of the BH5K running in a crowd of people breathing heavily in the first half mile! I breezed up the hill and enjoyed every step.

At the end of the race, about ¾ of a mile from the finish, we got to go down the same amount of elevation we had climbed at the start as we ran down a little hill approaching the University of Michigan's football stadium, the "Big House." We circled a small parking lot and then to my surprise we ran right down the tunnel normally taken by the football team to run out onto the field!

The finish line for the race was the 50 yard line and cameras were focused on us to put us up on the jumbotron just as we crossed the finish! People were jumping to hit the UofM banner as they crossed the finish. I missed that part as I was new at this and just focused on my running. We got our medals and they were giving out water after the finish line. What an inspiring re-introduction to running! When I caught up with my brother in law, I found out that his time got botched because he crossed the sensors twice! He had finished the race, then went back and ran with his wife across the finish line again and the system forgot his first time and kept the second one. This gave me a permanent phobia of walking anywhere near the timing mats after finishing a race with my chip on!

I liked the medal. Of course it was a maize and blue medal with a maize and blue sash.

I loved running Big House 5K so much, I got home after the race and immediately signed up for a race the very next weekend: the Martian Invasion of Races 5K in Dearborn.

Martian Invasion of Races

Parking in Dearborn can get a bit tricky, especially when there's thousands of extra people there for a race. And the Martian isn't just any race. It's a marathon, a half-marathon, a 10K and a 5K. I ran the 5K. So this meant I ran two timed races seven days apart. I got two finishers' medals seven days apart, and I must admit I thought the Martian medal was a lot nicer than the BH5K medal!

I loved running the Martian. Everyone along the sidelines seemed to have giant martian blow up dolls and a lot of runners were wearing silly outfits including tutus. I knew this would be a fun race when I noticed on the web site that "Scientists on Earth and Mars are working diligently to reduce gravity the day of the race." This was the kind of race I needed. It was tongue in cheek and a whole lot of fun.

After the great time I enjoyed at Martian, my run signup pattern continued. I kept coming home from one race and signing up for the next race that very same day. I grew close to several runners and we often shared rides to the races, especially if the races were a little further away. There were four of us that would often be seen at the starting line together, me, Tammy, Joyce and Natasha. Sometimes two others would join us, Terry and John. Not all of us could make every race. Joyce never wanted to run races on Saturday. Terry and John drifted away for a while. Natasha often had to travel for her job. Since most timed races were on Sundays, there were almost a dozen races that Tammy, Joyce and I ran together.

Apple Watch

When Apple Watch was announced, I ordered one 2 hours after ordering went live. I wanted to be able to check appointments, view texts and screen phone calls without fumbling for my iPhone 6. I was also interested in fitness apps that might be available on the Apple Watch.

For the first few months of running, I relied on my iPhone 6 and simple running apps like Runkeeper. Once my Apple Watch arrived, I switched to Runmeter because I liked the user interface better on the watch than the interface of any of the other apps I had tried.

I loved using my Apple Watch for runs. I was always wearing it so it was a simple matter to pull up the Runmeter app to start a run right from my wrist. There were difficulties at times and I relate these to issues related to the watch being a new product. Sometimes starting a run from the watch would simply fail and I'd have to start the run from my phone. Sometimes I'd have trouble stopping the run. Also it seemed like the GPS errors from the watch made all my run paces appear faster than I was really running. None of these were show stoppers as I was merely having fun and I didn't have any concrete goals just yet. One thing most apps had in common was automatic popups if I'd beat my previous best time for a certain distance. This is known as a Personal Record (PR).

There were issues with the Apple watch for me but I chose to ignore them. I liked having the "stand" reminders and I didn't mind at the time that the focus of the watch was more on being a smart watch than being a sports watch.

I was also running on days when I wasn't paying for races. My philosophy was to avoid running any distance for the first time "on the clock" so I'd practice every distance before actually going out and running it in a timed event. Tammy told me about a group run that took place every Thursday at Hansons Running Shop in Royal Oak. Every week, rain or shine, they run. I was intrigued and I went. I loved it and I loved the group dynamic. There were people of all abilities and all paces. There were incentives to keep coming back. After 10 runs you got a tech shirt. Free. After 35 runs, you got a nicer tech shirt. After 50 runs you got a free jacket. These were very nice perks and I decided to keep coming. I also liked the camaraderie of the group. When I first started coming, I was showing up in cargo pants and cotton t-shirts. I was running about a 10 to 11 minute pace when I was trying hard. I was averaging 3 runs a week and 2 paid races a month. I remember going around the Hansons 4 mile loop and thinking it was a challenge. I remember thinking that little incline between Vinsetta and 13 mile on Crooks was a "hill". I later learned what hills are at a route we like to call "The Seven Sisters".

The Hansons community of runners is a unique bunch of people. There are regulars that have been coming for over 250 runs. There are newbies who are there for their first group run. There are competitive athletes that routinely place in the top spot for their age group and sometimes win entire races. There are casual runners, like me, that are there for fun and camaraderie. Sometimes after a group run, there is pizza and often somebody brings craft or home brewed beer to share in the parking lot just as everyone is leaving. People bring snacks. People bring photos of significant events in their life. On warm summer days, it's not unusual to see 70 or more people at the Royal Oak store for a group run. On a cold snowy day in January or February, there are sometimes only a dozen or so "die hards."

Hansons Community Running Team is a way a lot of runners become more involved. Through HCRT membership, they get free or discounted entry into some of the races organized by East Side Racing Company (Hansons). They get discounts on shoes and clothing at Hansons stores. And there are several meetings a year where guest speakers come in to talk about training or other topics of interest to the group. Hansons hosts a number of regular runs. On Sundays, they offer a run from their Lake Orion store at 8am. On Mondays there are group runs from the Royal Oak store. On Thursdays they offer their largest group run from their Royal Oak store at 630pm. On Tuesdays during the summer, they offer speed workouts at Dodge Park in Sterling Heights at 630pm. Also on Tuesdays they offer group runs from their Grosse Pointe store. On Wednesdays they offer runs from their Utica store.

There are several special Hansons group runs that happen only once or twice during marathon prep season. The first of these is a Sunday morning 16 miler from the Grosse Pointe store that follows a magnificent course along the river. This usually happens in the fall as part of the Detroit Free Press International (Freep) marathon prep. In late March, there is a special version of the Lake Orion Sunday run that does 2 loops of the 7 sisters for a total of 16 miles. This run coincides with one of the last long runs for those preparing for Boston. These special runs get frequent water stations and even some crowd support. They are the best supported training runs I've ever seen.

Running Clothes and Shoes

The Martian Invasion of Races was the first real race expo I ever attended. Though I've been to many since then, it still ranks among the best I ever attended. First of all, there were vendors there selling running clothes and running shoes. Many of these were at a discount. A local store, Running Fit was selling a pair of top of the line Asics Nimbus running shoes for about ⅓ off so I bought them on the spot. I wore them for the Martian 5K and my toes got sore. I had picked them because they were the highest cushion shoe Asics made and I wanted comfort for these old bones. I wore them for a few more runs and I noticed toe pain. I had no idea why my toes got sore but I decided to look into different shoes.

This fit with my rule of solving any pain problems that came back day after day. On a Thursday group run night at Hansons, everyone who ran got a discount. I picked up a pair of Brooks Glycerin shoes and I loved them. They had more room in the toe than the Asics so I started wearing them for every run and my toes weren't getting sore any more. Changing to the Brooks Glycerin shoe solved the toe pain and I didn't consider wearing the Asics again. I think perhaps the sore toes were due to the relatively narrow construction of the Asics compared to the Brooks shoes but I bet my toes would have settled down if I'd waited a little longer. I still wear those Asics but only for walking. The Rockports I used to wear for walking now collect dust. Now when I hear somebody thinking of changing running shoes after only a few dozen miles, I advise them to give it a little longer for the shoes to break in, depending on the severity of the pain of course. But at this point in my running, I didn't know any better and the Brooks Glycerin provided a lot of cushion and were every bit as comfortable as the Asics had been so I never looked back. So this is an exception to my no pain rule. When it comes to running shoes, it's best to investigate pain before giving up on shoes too quickly.

I also wanted a pair of Gore Tex running shoes. I do live in Michigan after all and I really do like having my feet dry. Hansons was out of them. Brooks was out of them. Everybody was out of them so I resorted to Amazon and got a pair of 2014 Brooks Ghost GTX for what amounted to about ⅓ off. The GTX's were heavy shoes but I loved them.

I resolved to train in the GTX's and wear lighter shoes to race.

Clothing was a different matter. I normally wore cargo shorts and cotton t-shirts to run and this resulted in more than a few snickers whenever I attended group runs or a race. I noticed running apparel at Target was inexpensive so I picked up running shorts and tech shirts. I already had a growing collection of tech shirts that came with each of my races. Most of these were short sleeve so I picked up some long sleeve shirts. I also picked up a waist belt with a phone holder so I could have my phone with me on runs without it banging around in my pocket. I often found that I would make myself sore running by modifying my stride to keep the junk in my pockets from bouncing so much and driving me crazy. I recognized the need to run with as little as possible so I could focus on running and just plain relax.

Cotton doesn't dry as well as synthetic fabrics like polyester nor does it dry as well as wool. In cold weather it traps moisture and keeps it next to a runner's skin. There is a risk of hypothermia if a runner works out in cotton in the winter time and they don't put on something dry right away when they're done working out. One quote I remember about running clothes is this, "Cotton is rotten!" I had a lot of cotton things and little by little I began to replace them with wools and synthetics. I began wearing some of the many polyester tech shirts I was getting when I signed up for races. As I became more committed to running, I began to invest in better clothing and I was a regular customer at REI. I'll come back to this topic again when I discuss the clothing adjustments I decided to make after the Freep marathon and again when I discuss the resources I devoted to running.

Fr Richard Cassidy

In the winter semester of 2014-2015 school year, I took Pauline Scriptures at Sacred Heart Major Seminary with Fr Richard Cassidy. He is an awesome instructor who is passionate about scripture and has a gift for imparting understanding to his students. He got wind of my running and asked to see me after class one day. I had no idea what he wanted and I was so glad I stuck around. It turns out he has run ten Boston Marathons!

Fr Cassidy told me he thought I had what it takes to run a marathon. Then he showed me his marathon prep method aimed at first-timers. Basically it starts out with short runs alternating with short walks. It builds gradually to get you to over 30 miles a week. As you get closer to your marathon, he suggests you do a 22 mile run in the final weeks leading up to your marathon. It turns out I was already running over 20 miles a week "just for fun" so adding on more miles to prepare for a marathon didn't seem that daunting.

Still, I had to ask myself questions like, "Could I really do it?" "Do I really want to suffer like that?" "Is it safe or could I become injured by running too much?" So I took Fr Cassidy's advice and kept up my running but all along I thought the likelihood of me completing a marathon was pretty remote. He also shared a scripture with me from the writings of St. Paul, "I have competed well; I have finished the race; I have kept the faith." 2 Timothy 4:7. Another reading came to mind as I considered becoming a marathoner, "With God all things are possible!" Mark 10:27.

Cinco De Miles

In May of 2015, I realized I was getting pretty comfortable with running 5K races so I decided to try something new. I ran a race called Cinco de Miles in the early afternoon. This was my first race in the rain. The race was held in Dearborn and it was cloudy with a sprinkle here and there. It turns out I loved running in a light drizzle! Who would have known this could make running so pleasant. On very hot days, race organizers often put out misting stations for people to run through to get wet and help cool off. A light drizzle is the best misting station a runner could hope for. The only down side was my glasses were getting wet. I wished I had little windshield wipers for my glasses! I needed a hat with a bill to block the rain from going directly on my glasses, otherwise I was fine with running in a light rain. It turns out these are the best running conditions, light rain to cool you off during the rain but not so much rain as to create deep puddles and slippery spots.

After Cinco de Miles I headed over to Tammy's house to run another 5K with her. I felt fine. I ran 10K in one day with only a short break between those 2 runs to drive across town. I began to look for a 10K race to enter. In the back of my mind, a dangerous thought started simmering. Was Fr Richard right? Could I survive an entire marathon?

Komen 2015

I ran the Komen race again in 2015. It was one of the many races I found and signed up for now that I was enjoying running again. Only this time I invited my kids to run with me. When Liz arrived the morning of the race, she was surprised I had invited Tammy to run with us. Liz assumed we would be running just the three of us. Perhaps Liz felt that Tammy might attempt to "replace" her mother. This was the complicated landscape of our grief. I had focused on running Komen in Michele's honor and I hadn't given any thought to how my kids were feeling at the time. I merely assumed they would want to run for running's sake. I also assumed that they would enjoy the run. I came to realize that running a race to raise funds for breast cancer research so soon after my wife's passing from breast cancer came with some awkwardness that simply could not be avoided.

Again I was impressed with the crowd support and music along the course. The 2015 course followed along the river and was much more scenic and enjoyable than the 2008 course had been. I was disappointed that there were no timing results for any but the first few hundred runners. I understood that Komen was a fundraiser but how much does it cost to provide a time for each and every person who expends the effort to run 3.1 miles? Now that I'd run a few races and understood that chip timing was the norm rather than the exception. I had also read that Komen's administrative costs are high compared to those of American Cancer Society so I decided I wouldn't be running Komen again any time soon. I'd simply make a donation to ACS rather than jump through the hoops to run a race that wasn't really aimed at runners but was instead focused on fundraising.

My Decision to Sign Up for Freep

Commitment to More Running

I registered for the Freep Marathon on May 21, 2015. When I noticed it was to be held on the anniversary of my wife's funeral, I added the optional words "FOR MICHELE" to my bib and decided to run it in her memory. I knew I could change my registration to a shorter distance by paying a modest fee so I went for it. I purchased a copy of the Hansons Marathon Method on June 2, 2015 as I focused more intently on the feasibility of running an entire marathon.

I was enjoying running so immensely, I thought more is better, right? Well more water can lead to flooding, more sunshine can lead to drought and more running can lead to injuries. How fortunate I was that just as I was beginning to embrace running as a true passion, I had the benefit of a training program that has gotten athletes onto the

US Olympic marathon team in each of the past three Olympics. In 2016, an athlete made the Libyan Olympic marathon team using Hansons method, but I digress. In June of 2015, all I had was a vague desire to run a marathon, a paid registration for a full marathon with no obligation to run the whole thing (just yet).

I enjoyed the feeling of well being I was getting during and after runs. I was envious of the good experiences many of the Hansons runners spoke of when they talked about their marathons. I was also interested in someday running Boston. Someday. Maybe. So I was quite happy with my decision to register for Freep but I was uneasy about the commitment both in training time and effort. The next thing I wanted to try was doing longer races. I wanted to try 10K distances and longer.

Oak Apple Run

My first 10K run was the Oak Apple Run in Royal Oak. It was on the last Sunday in May and was actually after memorial day. I knew I had survived 10K in one day but I'd never kept going for an entire 10K race (since college). I ran a respectable sub 10 minute pace per mile and I was quite happy with the race. I loved getting medals at every race and I had several of them lying around from these earliest races. To me the cost of entering a race, roughly between $30 and $50 was not an issue. I enjoyed running with a group and I enjoyed getting an official time after each race.

Running in Korea

I kept running local races and joining the Hansons group runs every week. There were runs in scorching heat and runs in gentle rain. I really felt blessed that during my introduction to running, I was never asked to make a decision whether to go out in really inclement weather. That came later and I came pretty close to packing it in, but again I digress. As June wore on, the deadline to change my registration for the Freep marathon and drop down to either the US or the International half marathon was looming by August 26th. One of the things that was helping my decision was my ability to run an 11-ish minute pace "all day". My nephew Kyle had said "anything your body can do for half an hour it can do all day long" and that stuck with me. To me this meant that my enjoyment of 5K races were a sign that I could enjoy much longer distances as well.

During a business trip to Korea, I ran every day in downtown Seoul. Seoul has great places to run but at the time all I knew about was street running so I ran around a one mile block across from my hotel in the Youngdungpo area of Seoul. One day I felt particularly ambitious and I ran away from my hotel across the Han River to a park that had a 680 meter track and ran a lot of laps on the track before returning to my hotel. That day I did a full 16 miles at an 11 minute pace! To me this was proof that I could run "all day" and it helped solidify my decision not to change my Freep registration to a shorter distance. I began planning to go for it and I increased my running mileage a little each week!

Run Michigan Cheap Half

My first timed half marathon was put on by Run Michigan Cheap. They gave cotton shirts instead of tech shirts and they didn't offer chip timing but I was just running for fun and I had a running app on my phone that I trusted so I went and registered to run a half marathon on the Paint Creek Trail.

Paint Creek Trail from Rochester to Lake Orion is one of my favorite places to ride my bike so I was already familiar with it. I'd first learned about it when I had a friend from work who lived only a few houses from the trail at the Rochester end and we would go over to his house to park then ride the trail together.

I ran the Run Michigan Cheap half marathon on June 27th. This time I ran 13.1 miles at a 10:40 pace. The only thing I didn't like about Run Michigan Cheap is they didn't use chip timing. Their races were affordable but they used a timing system that was smartphone based and treated everyone's time as if they had crossed the start line together. Still, I was getting used to the idea that just about every time I laced up my shoes I would PR! This was intoxicating! I was satisfied that if I could run and enjoy a half, I could at least survive a full marathon.

Training for Freep

Hansons Marathon Method

Now that I was becoming more committed to actually running the Freep, I decided I had better find out what I needed to do to prepare. I wanted to not only finish, but finish standing up. I purchased a copy of the 2012 edition of Luke Humphery's "Hansons Marathon Method" on Amazon so I could read it on my Kindle and I devoured the book in less than a day.

I now realized that I had stumbled into a very unique situation. I was working with a group of people that wanted to bring running to the masses while at the same time they were working with elite and even world class Olympic caliber athletes. One of the points of Luke's book was that anyone could run a marathon when properly prepared. There were plans offered for anyone from a recreational runner to an elite athlete trying to qualify for the US Olympic marathon team.

As a new runner, I really didn't know what my potential was so I wasn't sure how to set my running goal. I decided I would pick a concrete goal of qualifying for Boston, (3:55) and work toward it. I was also interested in qualifying for London, (3:45) which was ten minutes faster than Boston and qualifying for New York (3:35) which was 20 minutes faster than Boston. Still, if I made my BQ time, I would have met my primary goal. About this time Tammy told me something she read in a magazine article, that a runner should **slow down in order to get faster**. At the time, I took this to mean I needed to make a serious effort to slow down for my recovery runs and I made an effort to make all my recovery runs significantly slower than my target marathon pace.

Mackinac Island

I decided to go "up north" for a week of vacation around July 4th. I put the dogs in the kennel, hopped in the car and headed north. I stayed at the Mission Point resort because the Grand Hotel was full. I planned on mostly goofing off during the week, but I also wanted to get some running in. It turns out these were some of the most pleasurable and memorable runs of my life. The weather was cool but not cold. The days were mostly sunny and for me there was plenty of goofing off stuff to do on the island. And there were no cars. Not one. Just people walking, bikes, dogs and horses.

The perimeter of Mackinac Island is just a little over 8 miles. I'd start from my hotel going north toward the sparsely populated part of the island then run all the way around and back to my hotel.

One day I rented a bike and rode around the island. It was a lot faster than running but I needed the training miles so on the following days I ran 8 mile loops again.

I stayed at Mission Point but I really wanted to eat at the Grand Hotel. Anyone can eat there but there is a dress code. I brought a sport jacket and tie for this purpose. I walked over and paid for dinner and enjoyed a fabulous 5 star gastronomic experience. After dinner, I spent a little time at a dance party they were throwing for hotel guests. Nobody looked at me for proof I was a guest because I was walking around in a sport coat like all the other guys. It was dark as I headed back to my hotel and I decided to get a cab, which on Mackinac is a horse drawn carriage available for a $5 flat rate per ride.

I would have to say 2015 was the year of "no rain on the days Jeff wants to do stuff" because while there was rain while I was at Mackinac, I never felt like I was pinned down or inconvenienced. I got all the running, bike riding, miniature golf, sightseeing, hiking and photography I wanted and I gave little or no thought to the weather.

As a runner, I had a real appreciation for the Apple watch. I could pull up the watch face, tap the current temperature and it would jump to a screen that had rain probabilities arranged around the clock face. I could see for instance that it was going to rain in 3 or 4 hours and decide to get my run in early or I might see that I could go out now in a drizzle or if I waited 3 or 4 hours there might be puddles still around but there was a 0 percent chance of rain. To me this hourly rain forecast on the watch face is one of the features that encourage me to still bring my Apple watch along on runs even if I chose not to use it for timing. On Mackinac Island, I used the weather info watch several times to adjust my run schedule to avoid rain.

Hansons Coaching

I signed up for Hansons coaching a mere 8 weeks before the Freep marathon. I decided that reading the book on my own and following along probably wasn't enough to guarantee me a good experience in a marathon. I really wanted to be prepared. At the time, Hansons coaching had several levels. I opted for the most affordable and I was assigned coach Katie Kellner. She loaded a training profile for me into Final Surge and I was on my way to not only running my first marathon, but running it well prepared. Or at least as prepared as I could be since I started formal preparation rather late.

One thing Coach Katie mentioned is that she wished I had signed up sooner as this really wasn't the normal 16 week preparation cycle. I was "cramming" my preparation by doing the last 8 weeks of the advanced profile. I told her I thought I could get away with it because my weekly running volume was up to 30 miles a week and I had been running for 4 months at the time I started working with her. I planned to run "as if" I had been doing that prep all along. This meant I started the preparation when workouts were switching from speed to strength and I never really got to work on speed. I also never got to gradually build up to the 50 to 70 miles a week recommended for marathon preparation.

Increased Running

I made a somewhat sudden jump from 20-ish miles per week to 40 plus miles per week. This most often leads to injury but in my case a higher power was looking out for me. This has been my running experience from day one. I have definitely benefitted from divine intervention as evidenced by my good health, good weather (most of the time), and stumbling into one of the best coaching programs available.

Coach Katie loaded a training plan for me that called for long runs on Sundays. The longest of these were 16 mile "marathon simulator" runs. These were designed to simulate the last 16 miles of a marathon because they were run on days when I had run as much as 10 miles the previous day. The program called for running six days a week. Long runs Sundays, easy runs Mondays, speed work or strength work Tuesdays, rest on Wednesdays, Tempo runs Thursdays, and easy runs on Fridays and Saturdays. I loved the way the Hansons method gave me "resting recovery" days between my tougher workouts. One thing I noticed was the cumulative fatigue effect. I was getting more and more tired as the training season wore on.

Summary Runs

Gophers and Founders and Heat

There were two races where we suffered in the heat. One was the "Gopher the Gold" 10K and the other was "Founders" 4 mile run. I was getting used to the heat but I got salt in my eyes at Gopher and I was glad when it was over. I went out and got one of those sweat band things after that race! Another hot as hades run was the Founders 4 mile race in Farmington. What an oven! The elite runners were all relaxing and enjoying it but those of us who were amateurs were taking it very easy and we were pouring water over our heads at the very first water station that day! High heat and humidity are not the runner's friends, especially if that runner is trying to go fast.

The weather wasn't always ideal for practice runs either. There were more than a few times I would show up for a run and it would be hot. Just. Plain. Hot. The first time I ran in high heat happened to be the first time I showed up for Tuesday speed workouts at Dodge Park with coach Dani Miller. Dani is one of the most enthusiastic running coaches I've ever dealt with and she makes

Tuesday speed sessions at Dodge Park a real pleasure. My coach had assigned about 8 miles of running but I did just over half that amount. It was my first speed/strength workout ever but I loved it despite the heat. I liked running fast but then being able to slow down and recover and then I enjoyed speeding up and running fast again. As I got used to the heat, I didn't mind doing my speed workouts in the heat of the afternoon so much and Dani always made sure to have a large container of water and plenty of pre-filled cups at the start/ finish line for each week's workout. We got crowd support and hydration at a practice run that was better than some races I've attended!

Hansons Tuesday speed work group at Dodge Park is an interesting mix of people. The elites don't always come to group runs but some of our stronger recreational athletes do come to speed work. Many of these runners can do sub 7 minute miles. Then there were the middle runners who ranged between 8 and 9 minutes a mile. And there are those who run over 10 minutes a mile. This means the group spreads out quite a bit over the curved trails at Dodge Park. Dani puts out cones to mark the beginning and end of intervals she has carefully measured with a wheel or other instrument. Running with such a diverse group means there is a lot to learn from other runners and there is almost always somebody running near my pace.

Hampton Virginia

There were a few other times I ran in high heat but they were "goof off" runs so I didn't mind so much. One was when I went to my goddaughter Rachel's wedding in Hampton, Virginia. I looked forward to seeing my best friends Ingrid and Michael at their daughter's wedding. It was so hot down there! I mean it was just hot. I went to mass in Hampton at a church where they didn't have air conditioning. Man it was hot! I got up and ran loops from my hotel, much like I had done in Korea but the sun was up and I was getting baked alive. I cut my runs short while visiting Hampton!

During this time I has having a tough time with family as we were all grieving Michele's passing in our own ways. It was particularly difficult with my daughter. There were times when she seemed to choose things to say to upset me and I couldn't perceive even the thinnest veneer or respect of daughter to father. So when Rachel started talking to Ingrid sounding just like Liz talking to me I began to realize that perhaps this was "normal" for millennials under stress and I shouldn't take it personally when Liz spoke in that tone to me. In fact it seemed that Rachel was extra nice to me and extra mean to her mother. This also reminded me of my experience with Liz. That visit to Hampton helped open my eyes and contributed to healing my relationship with Liz.

Rachel's wedding was held outdoors. In the afternoon. In the sun. I remember sitting in the congregation waiting for the arrival of the bridal party. We were sweltering in the heat and they were handing out chilled bottled water to everyone. When the bridal party arrived, they came in quickly. The minister said about a dozen words then Rachel and Allen recited their own vows which were also mercifully short. Then she pronounced them man and wife. This wedding was the shortest I'd ever attended. I think if it had lasted a second or two longer we would have had some heat stroke victims!

Arizona

As hot as I thought Hampton Virginia was, I ran in the hottest conditions ever when I visited Arizona in August. I would do my runs in the morning before the sun came over the mountains. I would start out when the temperature was just below 80 and the humidity was low. It felt like it was 60. But as soon as the sun peeked over the mountains, the temperature would spike and by afternoon it would be over 115 degrees. There was no way I was running in the high desert at 115 degrees! But those cool mornings in Arizona were almost magical. The cactus flowers were blooming brightly. There were mostly pinks and magentas but also some yellows. Some cacti were taller than me but most were close to the ground.

There wasn't much wind in the morning and while it felt cool with the low humidity and "only" 80 degree temperatures, I still had to do more than what I normally do for hydration. I was carrying water everywhere and I made myself drink frequently during runs. I would also drink several times an hour even if I had only been outside for a few minutes. I did one of those morning runs in an astounding sub 7 minute pace for 10K. At least the running app on my iPhone thought I did. I later took a look at the run and the GPS data was a series of zigzags all over the place. When I ran basically the same course the next day the GPS data was a lot smoother and it said I hadn't run as far. This means I probably ran a shorter distance the first time and the running app on the phone got "fooled" by intermittent GPS due to the mountains. I made sure I stayed in the shadow of the mountains when running in Arizona! Still, this apparently fast pace left me with the ambition to try to reproduce this result again.

Fall Runs

Detroit Women's Half Marathon Sep 2015

I did some of my Sunday long runs by signing up to run in local half marathons. One of these was a beautiful run held on Belle Isle called the Detroit Women's Half Marathon. This became one of my favorite races and my first experience with the magical effects of negative splits. I love Belle Isle and I'd always look for excuses to go there. When I saw there was a race there I immediately went to register. When I saw it was called the "Women's

Half" I decided to get on the phone and ask if men could sign up. The answer was yes! I signed up within seconds of hanging up the phone!

The Detroit Women's half was my first experience with trying to get to a race in a huge traffic jam. It seems the city of Detroit, in its infinite wisdom decided that the Sunday of the race would be a good time to close Jefferson Avenue. Completely. So the only way onto the island coming from the west was to go through the neighborhoods dealing with randomly placed one way streets and thousands of lost people trying to get to the same place. I'm a native Detroiter. I found my way through and got there in time for the start but the race started 20 minutes late so the rest of the runners could get onto the island. The weather was perfect. Not cold. Not hot. Not humid. Sunny and beautiful. This particular Sunday, I was planning to a 10 mile run so I worked it out with my coach that I would jog the first 3.1 miles and run the last 10 at marathon pace.

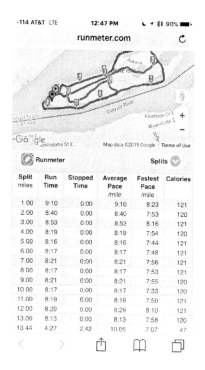

Split miles	Run Time	Stopped Time	Average Pace /mile	Fastest Pace /mile	Calories
1.00	9:10	0:00	9:10	8:23	121
2.00	8:40	0:00	8:40	7:53	120
3.00	8:53	0:00	8:53	8:16	121
4.00	8:19	0:00	8:19	7:54	120
5.00	8:16	0:00	8:16	7:44	121
6.00	8:17	0:00	8:17	7:48	121
7.00	8:21	0:00	8:21	7:56	121
8.00	8:17	0:00	8:17	7:53	121
9.00	8:21	0:00	8:21	7:55	120
10.00	8:17	0:00	8:17	7:33	120
11.00	8:19	0:00	8:19	7:50	121
12.00	8:29	0:00	8:29	8:10	121
13.00	8:13	0:00	8:13	7:58	120
13.44	4:27	2:42	10:05	7:07	47

That's just what I did. I started out running about a 9 minute pace. I ran with one group of ladies for the first 3.1 miles, talking and relaxing along the way. I explained that I would have to speed up soon. At 3.1 miles, I turned on more speed and started running faster than 8:30 a mile. I finished the half marathon with an average time of 8:30 per mile.

At the time, this was a PR for me. I had a habit of doing this. I would PR in practice runs and races that were being run as practice runs. In short, I was racing to train when I should have been training to race. Notice how much faster 8:30 is than 8:55? I did this all the time in my early training. I would rock practice runs and do just OK in races. I was later to appreciate that my tendency to "race to train" could lead to burnout.

Brooksie Way

The very next week after the Detroit Women's Half was another of my favorite half marathons, the Brooksie Way. In 2015 it included an evil little hill called Dutton. Oh yeah! This time my assigned distance was 16 miles so rather than run coast 3 slow miles and run 10, I had to run all 13.1 and add on 3 after the finish! This would later become my favorite distance: the 26K. So many of my weekend runs were on nice days. I think there were more nice weekend days during my marathon prep than I ever remember seeing before. It was just uncanny. There's a cliche about it raining on Sunday so you can look out the window of the office at the sun on Monday but I didn't have that experience even once.

The morning of the Brooksie way, the weather again was sunny and not too warm. It was just to my liking. Somebody up there was making sure I enjoyed running and I felt really blessed that particular morning. We started out from Oakland University's campus and ran through the neighborhoods toward another favorite running route of mine, the Paint Creek trail. We ran down Paint Creek trail and at about mile 8 we made a left onto... Dutton Road. At this point, picture the music from Jaws starting to play. At the base of the Dutton Road hill was a sign placed there by the Brooksie Way organizers which read: "This hill is steeper and longer than heartbreak hill in Boston." Nuff said.

I wouldn't say I powered up the hill but later when I analyzed my splits, I found I hadn't really slowed down that much at all. The hill itself is only about

¼ mile long but it's steep enough that it feels like you're walking when you go up, so for any split containing that quarter mile to only be off by a few seconds I must have been busting butt on that hill. There is a technique for tackling hills. That technique is "constant effort not constant pace." This is what I intended to do on Dutton but perhaps I was running a little harder than I intended. I remember hearing the breathing of runners around me and it sounded like steam engines about to burst. My goal in running was to never be so out of breath I couldn't carry on a conversation. I didn't always meet this goal and while I certainly didn't meet it on Dutton, I wasn't wheezing either.

At the end of Brooksie Way I picked up my medal but didn't stop the running app on my iPhone. I then started running around campus and tried to find the Brooksie Way 5K course. I found it alright and there were hills on that thing too! I didn't quite make 16 miles. I got to 15.5 miles and called it. I sent texts to Tammy and Joyce with my distance "15.5" and they thought I was sending them my pace! When we talked later I realized that simply sending 3 digits wasn't enough, I could have included "I did 15.5 mi" and it wouldn't have been that much harder to type and send. I was pretty tired after Brooksie but I felt good. Really good. The feeling you get after a hard run is something really special. It is a feeling of well being. The body has been doing what it was designed to do and it has been doing it well.

Sore Ankles

My favorite solo running course was across from my house. There was a sidewalk where you could run around the block and it turned out to be almost exactly one mile around. What was better was our sub had just signed a contract for snow removal for all of our sidewalks so this block would get plowed through the winter and remain a safe place to run without worrying about cars. I enjoyed running this loop because I didn't really have to think about anything at all. I just had to keep making left turns.

One day I noticed my right ankle getting sore and I attributed this to making too many left turns so I started doing half my laps one direction, then reversing direction for the second half of my runs. I did almost all of my easy runs using my neighborhood loop, and I also did quite a few of my long runs using the same loop. My neighbors all got used to seeing me running at all hours and they all asked me what I was training for. I found out that my neighbor Rod was training for the Chicago marathon which was a week before Freep. Sometimes he and I would be out running around the same time and we'd compare notes. He was focused on just finishing while I had a specific finishing time in mind.

One pain I had early on was Plantar Fasciitis. I had been wearing orthotic insoles since I started doing a lot of walking in 2012. My foot doctor prescribed them when I told her I was having heel pain. They provide a lot of arch support. Furthermore she told me not to lounge around with my shoes off but to keep on the shoes with orthotics. When I first started running, I put orthotics in my running shoes. This was a bad idea. Orthotics are hard plastic. When you take out the insole of a running shoe, you are losing a huge portion of the cushion designed to protect your joints. When you are running on a piece of hard plastic, your foot has a tendency to slide to the front of the shoe and your toes look terrible. Well it's not uncommon for runners' toes to look bad but when I was wearing those orthotics mine were particularly bad.

One day at Hansons, one of the visiting shoe reps mentioned that I probably shouldn't wear orthotics for running so I decided to see if I could get away without them. I was fine. So I had solved two types of pain. One involved running opposite direction laps on my neighborhood to solve ankle pain that might have been caused by always turning left. The other was getting rid of Plantar Fasciitis. I assume this was simply due to increased strength from all the running I was doing. All I know is the PF went away and didn't come back. At this point in my running, I only wore orthotics in my walking shoes. I never wore orthotics for running again.

Garmin

In the final weeks leading up to Freep, as colder weather approached, I found I had to run with long sleeve running shirts and jackets. I went on a long run at Lake Orion over the Seven Sisters and to my dismay, I would glance down at my Apple Watch expecting to see my pace and I would be greeted with... stock reports. Stock reports on a Sunday morning? There are no markets open on Sunday Morning and I'm out here to run not trade stocks! Then I'd try to swipe to get back to my pace and my fingers were too sweaty. Sometimes I was greeted with the passcode screen. Apparently my sweaty wrist, combined with the cool to cold conditions messed with the ability of the Apple Watch to remember it had never left my wrist. These issues meant I could no longer rely on my Apple Watch for running. I remember seeing almost all the other runners wearing dedicated running watches such as Garmin, Polar and others. I had tried my best to make do with my Apple Watch for running but as the weather required me to wear long sleeves for the foreseeable future, I decided it was time to declare the Apple Watch as a running watch experiment a failure. I bought a Garmin Forerunner 220 at REI and started running "two-wristed" in the final week leading up to Freep.

The Garmin came with a lot of great features. One was automatic upload of my runs to Garmin Connect and another was automatic upload of my runs to Final Surge so coach Katie could see my results and comment. Another feature was long battery life. Yet another feature was the ability to download complicated interval programs to the watch and it would vibrate and beep to let me know it was time to change paces. As much as I liked my Apple Watch, I had become very frustrated with its inability to lock the screen during runs so that long sleeves didn't make the watch go off into the weeds. I regretted not getting a Garmin sooner! The Garmin claimed everything I did was a PR because I hadn't worn it for any of my previous training.

One thing that occurs before a marathon is tapering. Put simply tapering means running a lot less. If you've been running an average of 50+ miles a week in training, the last week or two before the marathon, most training plans call for drastically reduced easier miles to be run. This allows the body to recover and rest up for the marathon but it also has an unintended side effect I like to call "tapering madness." It's more difficult to sleep when I haven't had a long run in days. I get irritable because running is, after all, an addiction and not getting any running can trigger withdrawal symptoms like irritability. Going into Freep I had my first real taste of tapering madness and I had varying degrees of friction with most people in my life including friends, family and coworkers.

Freep Marathon Oct 2015

Freep 5K

My running schedule called for a 3 mile "shakeout" run the day before Freep. For this run, I signed up for the Freep 5K run. This might have been a bit of a mistake because one should really rest the day before a big race and driving downtown early in the morning, looking for parking, getting in a start corral, all require effort even if the run is a mere 3.1 miles. I ran at the relaxed pace I was supposed to run but I was so distracted I even forgot to pick up my medal for the Freep 5K!

I had to choose a shoe to wear for the Freep. At the time I owned a pair of Asics Nimbus I was no longer using for running, and several pairs of Brooks shoes including Glycerin, Launch, and 2 pairs of Ghost GTX. I normally train in the GTXs because they are heavier and I wanted to run in a lighter shoe for the race so I wore the Launch. I also decided to wear some fancy compression socks that came up my calves. I had picked them up at the Freep expo. They were fifty bucks!

Running My First Marathon

Dark and Cold

Before dawn the morning of October 18, 2015, on the one year anniversary of my wife's funeral I was about to run my first marathon. I had decided to run in Michele's honor and had "For Michele" on my bib. My son dropped me off at zero dark thirty in downtown Detroit. I found myself standing in a huge crowd freezing in snow flurries. It was the coldest weather I had ever run in and I wasn't sure what to do. I wore several layers and because of the "bib rule", I assumed I couldn't do much to adjust my clothing during the race. Because Freep crosses an international border twice, runners must display their bib on their chest. This means if you have your bib pinned to your jacket you have to unpin it in order to take off your jacket and then pin it to the next layer. Some runners were running with bibs pinned to inner layers with jackets zipped open at the start. To me it was too cold for this. I wore two long sleeve tech shirts, an Arcteryx middle layer and a Mizuno wind breaker for my outer layer. While I was freezing at the time, I would find out later I had worn too much. My bib was green. Most others were blue. I didn't understand the significance of this until along the course I noticed people yelling "Good job, first timer!"

Quite a few of the experienced runners wore "disposable" hoodies they could discard at the start of the race. This is something I didn't know anything about ahead of time or I might have tried it. After the start, discarded sweats are collected and donated to those in need. I even saw a few runners with those tin foil wraps they normally give out at the end of races so they could keep warm. I was in the fifth wave which was fairly close to the front because I predicted my finish time as 3:55, in keeping with my BQ goal.

As each corral started, the remaining corrals moved up. Corral enforcement at Freep was on the honor system. I could have moved up or back if I wanted to but I wanted to stay near the pace team I needed to finish at my goal so I stayed put in corral E and waited for our start. The first corral to go were the quads. These were athletes on wheels. They were a lot faster on flats and downhills and a lot slower up hill. We would see them again on the bridge and yet again in the tunnel. The next corral to go was the elite runners. They were not using chip time. They were using gun time and were lined up across the start line. Next came waves B, C, D and finally my wave, E. There were at least 10 more waves behind us. There was about a 2 minute delay between waves. People were cheering. Everyone was excited. You would never have guessed that a few hours later some of us would be dragging our tired bones across the finish line looking like we just got released from a chain gang. It was all smiles at the start.

The Start

It was about this time that the sheer gravity of my predicament hit home. Like a little kid getting belted into a very fast very tall roller coaster, I realized I was not going to be able to get off this ride. The runners around me had serious expressions on their faces. I imagined it to be like soldiers on the eve of battle. I was there "just for fun" or perhaps "just to finish" and I was thinking "A BQ would be nice" but I was nowhere as serious as these people were. What on earth was I doing here?

When the time came for our corral to start, I found myself tripping over piles of clothing discarded by the earlier corrals of faster runners who had gone in the waves before us. I couldn't help but wonder how much harder it would be for the people in the back waves as the piles grew even taller! We ran into the darkness toward the Ambassador Bridge. The route proceeded more or less directly from Downtown Detroit through the streets to the bridge entrance ramp and our first hill. I wasn't sure what to expect but I thought perhaps I could run slowly up the bridge then speed up going down the other side for an average pace that was well faster than what I needed. I needed to run an average pace of 8:55 a mile for 26.2 miles but I found myself running 8:40 a mile in this early stretch. I started both my Apple Watch and my Garmin as I crossed the start timing mat but I glanced mostly at my Garmin's always on display to see how I was doing.

Canada

As we crossed the bridge, I was prepared for a beautiful vista but it was cloudy and still somewhat dark out so there wasn't such a great view. We ran into Windsor and the Canadian border patrol guys were all out cheering us on and joking with us about the Michigan Michigan State football game that had been played the night before. State had won to the annoyance of all the Michigan fans. In Windsor we had excellent crowd support. There were hundreds of cheering spectators in WIndsor and all of this was taking place during the first 10K of the marathon. We ran along the picturesque Riverside Drive and turned away from Detroit to go south toward the tunnel entrance. Yes only in Detroit is Canada SOUTH of the US, and you have to go further South away from the river to get to the tunnel entrance. I had heard about how hot it was down in the tunnel but I considered myself prepared. I was wearing a lot of layers but I could unzip layers to get more ventilation. I was also worried that I'd be breathing exhaust down there but there was no vehicle traffic allowed during the marathon so the air was reasonably clear. As I was in one of the earlier waves, I found that the air wasn't all that stuffy down there either.

At the middle of the tunnel, I got to the US and Canadian flags painted on the wall and I decided it was time for a photo. I tried snapping while running and that did not work at all. So I stopped and took a photo. This was one of the more enjoyable things I did. If I'm involved in an activity that is so intense I don't have time to stop, look around or take pictures, perhaps I need to be doing something else. At this point I was still with the 3:55 pacer and he was poking fun at me for taking pictures but this early in the marathon it seemed like I had infinite energy to spare. I chuckled and caught up with my pace group and continued up the spiral ramp and out of the tunnel. This is where a wave of cold air hit us just as we were sweating from being inside that tunnel. As we got to the top of the spiral ramp, I saw a couple dozen

US Customs agents standing at attention scrutinizing the incoming runners. This was not welcoming in the least and was nothing like the festive attitude I felt as we ran into Canada. As I felt the temperature changing again leaving the tunnel, I remembered that I could have and should have unzipped my outer layers. Oh well! We were a short distance from the half marathon point so I pushed on. At this point I was running ahead of my 3:55 pacer. Oh him! I never expected to see him again until he ran across the finish line behind me. Yeah, right.

Jealous

After leaving the tunnel we ran west on Jefferson under Cobo Hall and onto the Lodge freeway. We had taken over the Ambassador Bridge and the tunnel and we were also taking up a freeway! We took the first exit and ran back in the general direction of the bridge toward the Irish neighborhood known as Corktown. As we ran through Corktown the crowd support was present but very sparse compared to the turnout we enjoyed in Windsor. We then turned east once again and ran back past the start line where the international half marathon people were allowed to run into their finish chute. I remember being jealous of those half marathoners running into their finish chute and I was not happy that I wasn't finished running yet.

I was beginning to feel a little tired but I still felt like I could run forever. We ran to the east side of Detroit about ½ mile away from the river and about mile 16 we got to a beautiful neighborhood known as English Village. This was due North of Belle Isle and it was here I got my first inkling of trouble on the horizon. At mile 16 they were giving out beer. Beer? Heck yeah! Remember I wanted to goof around and not take this too seriously so when they offered beer at one of the aid stations I cheerfully took it and sipped a little. So far, at all the water and aid stations, I had tried grabbing a cup and drinking while I ran. This awkward maneuver actually wasted more time than simply stopping would have taken. I didn't know what I didn't know.

I Fall for the Wall

Shortly after the beer station, a small group cheering us on had erected a mock "wall" alongside the road. It was a painting of a wall with a little door for us to run through. I decided I was feeling so good I ran for it! I didn't notice that the curb was not a standard 4 inch city curb. It was more like 8 inches and I tripped over it and fell. I quickly got up and dusted myself off and rejoined my pace group. I resolved to never do a stunt like this again during a race as finishing strong was more important than tripping and falling for "stunts."

Throughout the race, I had been running ahead of my pacer and this was no exception. At about mile 18, I smirked and ran ahead of him and onto Belle Isle feeling like I didn't have a care in the world. Arriving on Belle Isle, I was now entering the last 10K of the Freep marathon and this was the last time I would be ahead of my pacer. He mentioned to me at that point that no matter how slow I thought I was running once I hit the island, I should keep running until the end. This unexpected statement got inside my head and I began to think some sort of surprise was in store on the island. Yes. There was a very unpleasant surprise in store. That wall I had been making fun of at mile 16 became a reality for me on Belle Isle.

Scott Fountain

As I rounded the turn to go past the Scott Fountain and approach the last 5K of the marathon, I suddenly became aware that I needed to shed every single ounce of weight I was carrying that was not essential. I started walking and dug my packet of Ucan out of my pocket and discarded it on the island. I had carried it thinking I could stop at a water station and mix and drink it but I had never gotten a chance. Now it was simply 8 very heavy ounces of something I no longer needed. I also threw away all those extra packets of goo I grabbed between miles 13 and 18. I didn't need any of them any more. I just needed to make it to mile 26.2. Alive. Another thing that hit at this time was the wind. No longer shielded from the cold wind by buildings, I was freezing with all those now sweaty layers on and I just wanted this thing to be over.

I was still within shouting distance of my pacer as we reached the Macarthur bridge heading off Belle Isle toward the last 5K of the marathon. This bridge has a very modest 10 foot rise over ¼ mile but to me it felt like I was climbing Mount Everest! I said goodbye to my pacer, knowing that I was going to be walking for "a while". I argued with my body and got it to start jogging again on the Detroit side of the Macarthur Bridge. Then there was a water station right about mile 23. Why not stop for water? I thought to myself. What a big mistake. I didn't start running again for another half a mile.

At this point, I realized why there are so few cameras and crowds between miles 20 and 26 of most marathons. Things get ugly! Things get really ugly! Runners are often walking or limping. I was increasingly confused and barely able to think. I could see the RenCen looming up ahead and even with less than 3 miles (5K) to go I wasn't quite sure how or when I would get there.

The Finish

Entering the last mile of the race I knew somebody was trying to kill me and that somebody was me.

I somehow got up the energy to kinda sorta jog the last ½ mile of the race so I'd at least LOOK like I was running. What I was really doing probably looked more like shuffling. I crossed the finish, glimpsing the timer that showed a time slower than 4 hours. I was angry that I had bonked but happy that I had finished. I got my medal and thanked GOD this thing was over. My time of 4:04:33 was respectable for a first marathon and while it was 9 minutes too slow for me to qualify for Boston, I decided it was close enough that I'd be able to figure out how to make it to Boston soon enough.

I wasn't really that sore, or so I thought. The race organizers provided a shiny silver blanket that I quickly decided I didn't need and handed it to my son to put in his bag for me. This was a big symptom that hits when I bonk. Mental confusion. During the "normal" part of the race, my thinking is clear. I can calculate paces, think about decisions, pray and remember which decade of the rosary I'm on and just generally function. Once I hit that super tired part of any race, I lose the ability to do much beyond focus on "getting this tired old horse to the barn."

The Freep medal was nice and heavy. It was much more substantial than any of the dozen or so medals I'd received for distances ranging from 5K to half marathon. It was the shape of an interstate road sign with red white and blue paint and a beautiful red, white and blue sash that had 26.2 printed so large you could read it across a parking lot.

I was able to walk fairly well and I wasn't taken away in a wheelchair or anything. My kids met me at the finish and we posed for a finish photo before we headed for the car. That's when they told me the car was in Greektown, over a mile away. I made a split second decision to stop in a nice warm Coney Island restaurant for a chili dog or three. I was hungry. Very hungry. My kids didn't understand. They had been sitting around while I had been burning close to 4,000 calories so they didn't get the whole NEED FOOD NOW thing. When we emerged from the restaurant, I was even colder than I was before and I started running. After running a marathon I was running to my car. It was stupid cold. This taught me an important lesson. BRING DRY CLOTHES. In cool or colder weather, never spend more than 30 seconds in the wet clothes you ran in. Ever.

Partial Victory

I had tasted not quite total victory but victory nonetheless. I had finished my first marathon! I had bonked and blown my time goal by 9 minutes but I still felt pretty good. I assumed my soreness was typical after running a marathon and I decided I would sign up for another marathon and try to make my BQ goal at the very next one. My BQ goal, for age 60 in April 2017 was 3:55. I had run 4:04:33. So I had only missed by 9 minutes even though I had hit the wall just after mile 20. I thought that if only I figured out how to avoid bonking at the end I would easily meet that goal. In this race I had begun to feel the wall at mile 21 and slammed into it about mile 23. I wanted to focus my training on moving the wall out beyond mile 25. If I hit at 25, who would care? I assumed that if I ran smart and had "banked" enough time, I would be able to walk the last mile and still meet my goal.

I also resolved to invest in better clothing as I attributed my bonk to two main factors, one of which was clothing. I was restricted to wearing a bib on my upper body and for this reason I didn't remove and add layers as I should have during the run. This resulted in a very sweaty run. The other factor was the restriction on bringing my own liquids onto the course. We were cautioned not to bring liquids across the border because Canadian or US Customs might take them away from us. I should have been able to bring my Ucan with me already mixed so I could just drink it to support my energy level during the run. Notice how I'm blaming stuff that had nothing to do with physical training? I assumed I was strong enough and that the reasons I didn't run well were external. There was some truth to these assumptions but in hindsight I think there was a third factor, I hadn't done a rigorous full cycle of marathon training. I had simply started the last 8 weeks of the advanced training regimen and pretended that the goof off running I'd been doing leading up to that point was "roughly equivalent" to what I would have done if I'd been following proper training all along. Not even a little bit true.

Part 3

Training for Disney

Health Assessment

Korr VO2max Testing

I decided my next marathon BQ attempt would be the Disney World Marathon, January 10, 2016. This meant my training would have to start up just after the 2 week embargo after Freep was over. This suited me fine as I'd rather run than not run. I told coach Katie I was planning to run Disney "for fun" and I asked her to review and comment on my runs but I didn't ask her to load a plan for me. Meanwhile, I started looking into a way to diagnose what my actual capabilities might be. I not only wanted to squeak by my BQ time (3:55), I wanted to qualify as "Good for Age" for London (3:45) or even qualify for New York (3:35). I started looking for VO2max testing. I had heard anecdotally that it is possible to predict a runner's fastest race performance based on their current cardiovascular fitness. VO2max testing consists of running on a treadmill at an ever-increasing incline while an EKG is being recorded. Between incline increases, blood pressure is checked. This test can be done at a number of places, often at a local gym.

I went online and found 2 candidates for my testing. One was Beaumont Cardiovascular Performance Clinic. Another was a local gym that I only went looking for when Beaumont was unavailable. When I called Beaumont, they said the soonest I could get in was February 2016 which was a month after my marathon! I asked to be put on their wait list and I started looking for another option. I had followed a link from a company that makes VO2max testing equipment (Korr) and found a local gym that could run the test and they could get me in on a few days' notice. The total cost was around $100. I jumped at the chance and signed up.

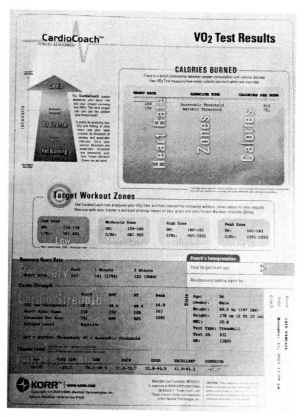

The person administering the test, Anthony, was an athlete and a coach. He was the owner of the gym and explained very clearly what the test would be like. There are several versions of VO2max or stress testing. One method, called the "Bruce" method involves increasing incline to a very steep angle while moving at a constant rate of about 5 mph or a 12 minute mile. Each incline increase lasts 3 minutes. There were a couple of spots where the assistant asked if we should stop the test as my heart rate shot up past 170 but Anthony understood how runners fare on these tests and let the test go. Sure enough after a few seconds my heart rate decayed back down sub 140 after each increase in incline. At one point I grew tired and was ready to stop the test. I made it to stage 4 and had a VO2max that was about 54.

The next thing I was expecting was a cardiologist consultation. I was referred by the local gym to a doctor who had at one time been the director of the Beaumont clinic. I scheduled an appointment with him and thought I was on my way until I got a call from his office explaining I needed to pay a hefty fee up front to see him and any additional testing or visits would be over and above this cost. They also let me know he didn't take insurance so this meant dealing with claim forms. I canceled the appointment. I thought I would really like this cardiologist, but he turned out to be more of a concierge cardiologist and this was a level of service I couldn't afford. I had a VO2max number but I still hadn't consulted with a cardiologist about my desire to run marathons for the first time as I approached age 60. I was also concerned that the report didn't clearly break down target heart rate zones. Each of the 5 heart rate zones on the report were only a few BPM wide. To me, the report should have showed a recovery zone that was about 60% of the heart rate it was showing for the highest intensity zone. The peak zone was 162 to 163 or only 1 BPM wide. How could I use such a narrow target to set my exercise goals? I decided to simply use the number "54" as an indicator that I was in excellent cardiovascular health and ignore the rest, for now.

My Doctor

I went to see my primary care doctor because it was time for my annual physical. My doctor is patient and spends a lot of time with me at each physical. This year I had taken a cholesterol screening at work that showed me to have levels that were near normal. I shared with him that I had stopped taking my meds as my running volume had ramped up. Part of my incentive for running was to eliminate the need to use drugs to control my cholesterol. He reluctantly agreed to let me stay off the drugs provided the results from the test I took that day weren't too high. I was elated. In my quest for good health, I really wanted to stop taking any medications that weren't absolutely necessary. I still take over the counter antihistamines for my seasonal allergies but I have no prescription meds whatsoever.

During this visit, my doctor asked me to stop running. He said I was too old to run. I said "No I'm not too old and I'm not about to stop running!". He then asked me if I was addicted to running. I cheerfully said "Yes, I am!". There are recovery programs for people with addictions to things ranging from substances to behaviors like gambling. The one mark of a true addiction is unmanageability. If I was missing time from work and, or paying bills on time, or neglecting my family to run, or running despite injuries, I would certainly consider quitting. None of these were true. I was feeling better than ever and running was helping me work through grief after the loss of my wife. I was not about to quit and I let him know I could find another doctor if he was really serious about me quitting. He backed down.

Beaumont Performance Clinic

A few weeks after the local gym test, I got a call from Beaumont that an opening was available so I took it. I didn't mind paying for another test because I never got the cardiologist consultation that I wanted to go over my previous results. Beaumont was more expensive but I would get an ongoing EKG during the test, and I would get an ECG (Electro Cardiogram - Ultrasound of the heart) separately and the cost also included a cardiologist consultation. At less than $400, I didn't mind paying for the second round of testing.

I arrived at the Beaumont clinic in loose-fitting cargo pants and I had forgotten my belt. I got on the treadmill for this slightly different version of the "Bruce" stress test. A lot of people hear stress test and think of something awful but for a runner and especially for a marathoner, a stress test is pretty much a non-event. Once again my heart rate shot up at each incline and each pace change but decayed back to sub 140. This time the tech had to hold up my falling pants so I could focus on running. Here was another lesson learned! Never wear loose clothing to a run again. Not even a treadmill run! During this second VO2max test in as many months, I still made it to stage 4 with an 18 percent grade and 12 minute pace for a VO2max of about 48. While slightly lower than the result from the test at my local gym, VO2max was still considered superior for my age, only this time I was about to get a lot more useful information than a mere number. **My VO2max of 48 corresponds to a METs of 13.5 and a calculated race pace of 8:31 to 9:15 without lactic acid forming.** This is vitally important to marathon and ultra runners. We have to figure out how to run long distances without waking up those muscles that deplete glycogen stores and form lactic acid. If we can avoid waking that sleeping dragon, we can run "forever" such as a half-marathon, marathon, or even an ultra-marathon race. The formation of lactic acid is what causes pain during running. My running motto was, "No pain, NO PAIN!" so I was delighted somebody was handing me a formula for (near) total pain avoidance.

Tracking VO2max

During my investigation of my VO2max, I added columns to my tracking sheet to calculate VO2max based on my training run or race performance for each day. I used the Daniels and Gilbert formula widely available on the internet...

$$VO_2Max = \frac{0.000104v^2 + 0.182258v - 4.6}{0.2989558e^{-0.1932605t} + 0.1894393e^{-0.012778t} + 0.8}$$

As is often required with these formulas, I had to do some unit conversions. Garmin is able to report distances in meters but I prefer miles. Of course the formula wants velocities in meters per second, not minutes per mile or miles per hour. The formula in my google sheet looks rather ugly but it works...

```
=if(C95>0,(if( F95>0,
(-4.6+0.182258*F95*26.8224+0.000104
*(F95*26.8224)^2) / (0.8+0.1894383
* 2.71828^(-0.012778*C95*24*60) +
0.2989558 *
2.71828^(-0.1932605*(C95*24*60))),"
")),"  ")
```

The if blocks prevent my spreadsheet from being populated with hundreds of calculation errors for runs I haven't completed yet. As soon as I enter the Garmin data for a given run, the VO2max shows up. My calculated VO2max for Freep was 37.1. Looking at the formula, velocity squared appears on top so running faster helps raise VO2max. There are two e to the minus t terms on the bottom so running longer helps raise calculated VO2max. Running a 9 minute mile in a marathon indicates a lot higher VO2max (39) than running a 9 minute mile in a 5K (33.5).

Practice Runs for Disney

Fatigue

I decided to duplicate the training I had done for Freep to prepare for Disney but I also decided to "add on" miles to be better prepared. I didn't ask Coach Katie to load any specific planned program for me as I believed I could simply repeat the one I had just completed and I'd do fine. In my mind, I wanted to get BQ out of the way in January so I could spend the bulk of 2016 doing "goof off" runs. In the Hansons method, you are discouraged from adding miles on Long Run days. It's always better to add miles on recovery run days. I did this a lot. But I also ran too fast. I prepared as if I was expecting to run 8:40 a mile rather than 8:50 a mile. In fact, some of my runs were paced such that I was preparing to run 8:20 a mile. This meant I dealt with a lot of negatives all at once. My cumulative fatigue was too high, daylight was becoming scarce and running conditions were becoming downright dangerous between snow and ice on the roads.

I was running while holding a full time job so my runs almost always were in the dark. It sometimes seemed like drivers were trying to hit me despite all the reflective gear and LED lights I was wearing. One day I took my car in for service at a local tire store during a blizzard. I asked how long the repair would take and they told me 90 minutes. I was wearing my running stuff so I left the car with them and ran out the door through the rapidly accumulating snow. It snowed 11 inches that day and I ran through the peak of the snow storm. I loved it but I think running in conditions like this can lead to burnout and I probably would have been better off waiting for better conditions.

Turkey Trot Drumstick Double

As part of my Disney prep, I signed up for a 15K race. This was the Detroit Turkey Trot "Drumstick Double". You had to run the 10K then make your way back for the start of the 5K run. They ran the 10K first because it used the entire parade route and they wanted us out of the way so they could get the parade started on time. The 5K was run only on the southernmost part of the parade route so it could start later.

After my freeze, bake, freeze cycle at Freep I decided to invest in more specialized running clothes for cold weather. The most urgent category was a base layer. There are several brands available. I picked up Smartwool and Arcteryx base layers. I found these to be invaluable when running on colder days and even though it wasn't as cold as some Thanksgiving mornings in Detroit can get, I was glad I had them in time for Turkey Trot. I had also invested in replacing all cotton underwear with polyester. I still had a few pocket t-shirts lying around for everyday use but I never wore cotton again for a run.

Thanksgiving morning 2015 was a cool morning but not outrageously cold. Thanksgiving morning in Detroit can be bitter cold. In 2013, my friend Robert invited our family down to view the Thanksgiving parade from the Whitney restaurant. The Whitney served a delicious brunch and after we had eaten our fill, we went out in front of the restaurant to sit on dedicated bleachers under warm blankets to view the parade. With our winter coats on, sitting under blankets we still froze and about ⅔ of the way through the parade we opted to go watch the rest from back inside the restaurant. This memory was fresh in my mind as I arrived downtown for the turkey trot and I was so happy the temperature was a moderate 48 degrees rather than something below freezing.

Tammy and Joyce were with me and we went to a coffee shop called Roasting Plant. They have delicious coffee, but it's pricy. One blend they have costs over $80 a pound! We walked around the start area looking for some women Joyce knew that are members of the Black Girls Run group. We found them and took several group photos before it was time for me to peel off and get to the start corral for the 10K. I set a personal record for 10K at that run of 7:45 a mile for 6.2 miles. Then I went and got in the queue for the 5K and ran an 8:27 pace in that race immediately after my PR in the 10K. Based on this time, I began to think I could go faster than my goal pace of 8:55 a mile and I decided to train at faster speeds as well as add on miles to train for Disney.

Seven Sisters

During my Disney prep, I found a new course to run on that I really loved. I fell in love with the Hansons Lake Orion Sunday morning run over the seven sisters. This route takes you out of downtown Lake Orion around a loop that includes some steep hills. The Sunday group run turnout is usually at least 20 runners and it's an even larger group the last Sunday of the month when another local coach, Bruce, brings his runners. After the run, I enjoyed going to CJs diner for breakfast, especially if it had been a long run.

The Seven Sisters route is 9 miles long and includes about 350 feet of vertical climb which is considered good strength and stamina training. There is a variation where you do two loops of the sisters (hilly portion) for a total of 16 miles by the time you get back to the running store. There are other route options available. One of these is the "Drahner" loop that adds on about a mile and a half but also adds 250 feet vertical for a total of 500 feet vertical for the entire Drahner loop. The Drahner loop takes you past the highest point in Oakland County and you run past a Benedictine monastery at the very top. They affectionately call this route "Mama Drahner and Her Seven Brats." At this point in my running, I didn't bother with the Drahner loop. I was happy enough to finish a loop (or two) of the Seven Sisters.

Zen and Yoga, Prayer and Mindfulness

Meditation During Runs

For me, running was always a meditative and perhaps even contemplative activity. I knew intuitively it was helping me process my grief over the loss of Michele. It was giving me quality time doing self care. I had neglected self care when I was her caregiver during her illness and now running gave me time to take care of myself. I would pay attention to my body. My breathing. My soreness and how I felt in general. Tammy mentioned a book she had read that she really enjoyed by Robert Persig. It was called "Zen and the Art of Motorcycle Maintenance". It was a great if somewhat difficult read. There were two stories. One was the story of the author's motorcycle trip across the country with his son. They experienced various mechanical breakdowns, weather problems and the like. This reminded me of the trials and tribulations of long distance running. Another story in Zen was the struggle in the author's mind about the nature of quality. Here he delved into the ability to know anything at all. Philosophers call this topic ontology. He was living with a part of himself bottled up and he was afraid to face it. This was something I could relate to during my period of grief. Zen was one of the books I read recently that changed my life. I found it easier to focus my attention on here and now and on things that really matter. I found it easier and easier to let go of things that did not or no longer mattered.

Yoga Classes

I made another discovery during my Disney prep, Yoga. My gym offers yoga lessons every day and some of the scheduled times occur at times I can actually get there. Tammy invited me to a Yoga studio in downtown Royal Oak and I bought a single introductory pack of lessons. I was amazed how many marathoners where there! It seems like Yoga was one thing I was missing in my prep for Freep that I would now have going into Disney. I found that some of the stretches were helping with my spinal alignment. When I went to see my chiropractor before leaving for Disney, he reported everything was in alignment. He made a couple of minor adjustments but going to Yoga frequently during training kept me from having to see him quite as often for adjustments. And when I did get chiropractic adjustments they were minor.

The philosophy of Yoga became important to me as well. During Yoga practice, it is important to focus on the here and now. Like the message that came through loud and clear when I read Zen, I was hearing that being in the present is an important thing to practice. This was a lesson reinforced when I read "Peace is Every Breath" by Thick Naht Nanh. Yoga had gotten me thinking about my breathing the here and now, as had Zen but Thick Naht Nanh's accessible approach to contemplation gave me even more of a glimpse of what life is like when a person is mindful. As I approached the Disney marathon, I began to practice mindfulness in earnest.

Grief Support

One of the factors that got me ready for the huge change in my life going from no running at all to marathon was grief. I visited local grief support meetings and read some very good books on grief. One book was CS Lewis' "A Grief Observed." I had underestimated how big a deal it is to lose a spouse and when I read what CS Lewis went through even though he'd been married only a short time, it allowed me to give myself permission to deal with my grief on my own terms, at my own pace and in my own way. An important part of my way of dealing with grief was through running. While thinking about writing my story, I considered whether I was running away from something or to something. Perhaps I was running away from the pain of grief. Perhaps I was running toward forgetting a sense of loneliness after 25 years of happy marriage. As I reflect now, I think I was running into the arms of a grief that helped me become a better person.

I've had to deal with death more than most people I know. I've never been in war, but I've lost people close to me quite a few times. When I was only 19, I lost my father. This was devastating to me. I cried and cried. I was a college freshman at the time and I took "a few years off" collage afterwards. Some years later, after I finished college and was established in my career, my mother remarried. My stepdad passed about 10 years after that. My mom married a third time and this time my stepdad died exactly a year later on their anniversary. My mom passed in 2005 and by then I was getting jaded. I had grown up an only child until my mom's third marriage but I then had 6 adult siblings. After my mom died, my brothers Gerry and Delbert passed. I was becoming too well-versed in how to arrange funerals, pick readings for the service, talk to funeral directors and so forth.

When my wife passed, I didn't process the grief in any way I expected to. I had a lot of energy and questions whirling in my mind. Running had begun to help me deal with my grief as well as deal with those around me who were grieving including my adult children and my wife's siblings. When a friend suggested I attach goals to certain races or even certain hills during runs, I thought this was a wonderful idea. I would pick an upcoming hill and say, "By the time I crest this hill, I will have come to terms with my identity as a single man" or "I will have forgiven so and so for such and such." These were largely symbolic, but they helped me achieve a certain amount of inner peace, in spite of the turmoil of my grief.

Prayer

Another habit I began to develop was prayer while running. This was helpful in a number of ways. First of all, I had set a personal goal to increase my prayer time. Second of all, if I was becoming exhausted which was quite common for me after about 13 miles, I would get all mixed up and have to keep starting over. For instance, if I was praying the rosary, I could count 10 Hail Mary's on my fingers easily enough but if I kept forgetting which mystery I was on, I knew I was becoming exhausted. Awareness that I was losing track either of my train of thoughts or of the prayers I had decided to say helped me with mindfulness. It served as a warning that I was pushing too hard during a run.

This habit of praying during a run is helpful when running alone. I find that when running with a group, if we are going at a relaxed enough pace to allow talking I merely focus on the conversation and pray some other time.

Disney Marathon

Orlando

I arrived at Disney World a week before my race which was scheduled for Januray 10, 2016. I planned to do my last few runs in Florida, including a dirt road that winds through the orange groves to the west of Orlando. This dirt road course was also used by the Hansons elite athletes who would be in Florida for six weeks preparing for Olympic marathon trials coming up in mid February in LA.

I checked in to one of Disney's "value" resorts and resolved to stay away from the amusement parks and just focus on my running. I was sick when I landed in Florida. I had caught a cold as I approached the end of my Disney marathon prep and I was not one bit happy. In the warmer temperatures of Florida, I started feeling better day by day.

I was staying at one of Disney's All Star resorts which means I was very close to the marathon start, I was close to the Expo which was being held at Disney's ESPN Sports complex and I was close to the southern border of the Disney property. There were a couple of down sides to choosing the more modest resort. There weren't any indoor seating areas to simply relax and read and Disney's value resort dining options were limited to cafeteria or counter style service. Inclement weather would mean I was either in my room or in the large cafeteria area. Given a choice, I prefer table service to cafeteria service. Since I was there to focus on my running, I didn't mind this so much but perhaps I'll go for a little higher end room the next time I run Disney.

I went to Downtown Disney several times during my week at Disney World. It is basically a shopping district but it shares the meticulous attention to detail as the parks that require admission. I didn't want to pay admission and feel compelled to cover a lot of ground and thereby tire myself out so I stuck to things I could do for free. I also visited Old Town Kissimmee which is a small shopping and amusement district not far from Disney property. There are a number of souvenir shops and a few attractions that charge a modest admission. My week was spent reading books on my Kindle and browsing things I could either drive a short distance to see or reach on Disney's transit network. I ate at Animal Kingdom Lodge one day. The meal was tasty and I was glad I made time to get over there and eat. I visited a part of the complex where giraffes wander freely and can walk up to the balcony of the room and kids can feed them right from their hotel room. Those rooms cost $800 a night. Yikes! Each day I ran the 5 or 6 miles my tapering run schedule called for. Most often, I ran this on the path right outside my hotel which was clearly marked for a mile of running so I'd go up and back a half dozen times and I'd be done. Sometimes I'd add on using not so well marked trails bordering employee only areas of Disney. One of these took me past beehives where I wouldn't doubt the Disney beekeepers are able to harvest a lot of honey.

The Expo

The Disney marathon expo was easily the largest I'd ever attended. It turns out there are over 72,000 runners considering all the events.. And there are two challenge races for the very physically fit, or perhaps very mentally unfit. There is the Goofy challenge which is the half marathon one day and the full marathon the next day. Then there is the Dopey Challenge which consists of distances doubling every day for four days from 5K Thursday, 10K Friday, half-marathon Saturday and full marathon on Sunday for a total of over 48.6 miles.

Jeff Galloway was there promoting his run-walk method and I got a photo with him. This method is remarkable. If you want to finish a marathon. Just finish. And you don't care about your time. Go ahead and sign up for one. Only mix running and walking so your body never enters the fatigue zone and you will wind up with a finisher's medal just like the guys who ran the whole thing. I bought one of his timers and I bought a copy of his book to read on my Kindle. This was only my second marathon and I still didn't fully understand how to finish a marathon properly, without soreness, bonking and fatigue. I knew from Freep that "something went terribly wrong" on Belle Isle after mile 20 but I still couldn't put my finger on it. I was intrigued by the possibility that someone who was only moderately prepared for a marathon could finish comfortably and even run frequent marathons without risk of injury.

Galloway's method consists of alternating running and walking throughout the entire marathon rather than just at the end where you typically see the "bonkers" dragging their feet. This keeps a runner's heart rate lower and helps endurance. One example is run 2 minutes and walk 1 minute. Another example is run 8 minutes and walk 30 seconds. I opted for the something closer to the latter. I would try to "stack the deck" toward success by walking every single water station. The longer the walk interval, the faster you have to go during the run interval so to avoid having to exceed the paces I had trained for I opted for a very short walk interval. One thing I did not want to do was attempt something new at the marathon I that had not perfected in practice. I planned that I would only walk the water stations so I wouldn't be choking down liquids at a jogging pace and I would still benefit from the lowered heart rate a 20 second or longer walk provides during a race. This was one of the keys of the Galloway method. You could walk longer but the practical minimum walk to achieve benefit was about 20 to 30 seconds or about the time it takes to relax and drink a few ounces of liquid at a water station.

I spent a lot of time at the Expo as it was something I could do for free during my week at Disney and it went all week long thanks to a 4 day racing schedule. There were panel discussions by Runner's World writers. There were booths set up for everything from specialized running clothes and socks to nutrition supplements designed to be eaten during the run. There was a group from Garmin including a guy who knew a thing or two about Garmin engineering. I found out that the newer Garmin models with heart rate in the wrist have gone through 2 iterations. The first iteration used a sensor Garmin outsourced from Mio while the newer iterations were using Garmin's own sensor. I had invested in a Garmin chest strap during my Disney prep and I hated putting the thing on, especially in winter. Often I'd be getting ready to run and I'd already have a base and middle layer on then remember the doggone strap! I put a newer Garmin with wrist-based HRM on my list of things to buy "someday soon."

Every shoe company was represented at the Disney expo, but New Balance enjoyed prominent placement. Tammy had expressed interest in the Nike Pegasus shoe and I spent some time at the Nike booth and at the Nike outlet store looking at this shoe. The Nike outlet store was somewhat comical. You could have discounted Nike shoes as long as you didn't mind that the only color they had in stock was bright orange. Yikes! I owned several pairs of Brooks shoes, Mizuno, Asics and even one pair of Newton trail shoes but my favorites were my Brooks. The Brooks felt most comfortable and the only point of dissatisfaction was the lack of variety in "drop". Drop is the distance of the heel above the midsole or toe. I routinely switch from high drop (10mm or more) to low drop shoes (6mm or less) for my various runs. Getting a low drop shoe that wasn't going to cause me any pain was a priority for me.

At the time I only owned one pair of "low drop" Brooks shoes, my Pureflows, but I didn't find them comfortable. In fact more often than not, I'd have a sore back after running in them. I went to the running store at Downtown Disney and had them film me wearing my Pureflows on their treadmill and then film me wearing the new 2016 model. What a difference. The 2015 model didn't seem symmetrical in the heel area. It seemed like somebody had taken a knife and chopped off part of the heel so that if you stood erect with weight on your heels, your feet naturally tended to roll out with your inside toes lifting off the ground. As a heel to midfoot striker, this was making me sore. I asked the Florida Brooks rep at the Expo if I could return my 2015 Pureflows for the newer model and while he couldn't speak for the Michigan rep, he said if I did it in Florida it would be fine by him. I put this on my list of things to do when I got back home. I would trade in my 40-ish mile 2015 Pureflow 2s for the newer 2016 Pureflow 3 model. One thing I think helps my running is using a variety of shoes. I want shoes with different "drop" heights, different cushioning and different weights.

Running Disney

The Start

When the morning of the Disney marathon arrived, I disliked having to get up so darn early to catch a 3am shuttle to the start of a 5am race. I had stocked up on Bear Naked Maple-icious Pecan granola and almond milk and that's what I had for breakfast before leaving to catch the shuttle. It had been pretty warm all week but I assumed that this early in the morning it would be pretty cool so I dressed for warm but not hot weather running. I took 3 pairs of shoes with me. I took my go to shoes, the GTX's just in case I had to run in a downpour. I took some almost brand new T7 racers and I took my Launch that had served me so well in the Detroit marathon. This time I tried some new compression socks. Instead of the ones that went halfway up my calf, I opted for compression socks that went just up to my ankle. I decided to wear the T7 for the Disney Marathon because they were the lightest shoes I owned at the time. I wore the T7s and caught the shuttle bus from my hotel to the start of the race.

When I arrived at the start, I began to have an appreciation for the scale of the Disney marathon. In Detroit, all the corrals had fit in about a 3 block area downtown. At Disney, the corrals stretched for almost a mile. There were tens of thousands of runners. Corral placement was strictly enforced. You couldn't move up but you could move back. And you had to submit race results to justify your corral placement. Since my Detroit race had taken place after the stated cutoff date for corral placement, I had some anxiety about whether they would put me in the correct corral or not. I also asked myself why anyone would want to move back and possibly get hung up behind a bunch of walkers and made my way to the front of my corral. I was delighted I was in the 9 minute mile corral and not back there with the 15 minute mile people.

Heat, Humidity and Pace Warning

Jeff Galloway got up and made announcements at the start of the race. One announcement caught me by surprise. He strongly recommended running 30 seconds slower than our target pace due to heat and humidity the day of our race. To me this would be a let down because I secretly wanted to BQ at this race so I could relax the rest of 2016 rather than continue the rigorous training I was doing toward a BQ marathon performance. Coach Katie had advised me to treat this as a "fun" marathon but I would have been delighted to put the whole BQ thing behind me at Disney. I knew we were getting close when they sang the national anthem. As they let the first wave go they set off a barrage of fireworks. I thought they would only do this once but they did it again for every wave including mine. I was in the fourth wave and I got to see four fireworks shows that morning.

Magic Kingdom

We ran out into the darkness from the start area toward the entrance of the Magic Kingdom park.

Cinderella's Castle was covered with green LED's. I stopped a few times and took photos. I now had the attitude that I was going to enjoy every run, photos and all.

I had decided that the first priority for me in running any distance was enjoyment from start to end and if I had to formally adopt Galloway's method I would. Of course I hadn't practiced Galloway's method preparing for Disney so I didn't focus on using it. I had his timer but I didn't turn it on and try to use it. I did begin to think about saving myself for later rather than running harder at the beginning when I was feeling a burst of energy. Leaving Magic Kingdom, I put my mostly run but walk a little from the very start plan into practice. I ran a little faster than my goal pace but I walked each and every water station. I had promised my coach I wouldn't go out "too hot" so when I saw my splits were too fast, I walked a little slower to try to keep my pace down to what it should be this early in the race.

I wasn't using one of Jeff Galloway's recommended ratios but it served my purpose of making the marathon easier on me without slowing down too much. More importantly it didn't require me to run faster than my recommended pace to compensate for longer walking intervals. The mile markers were a little off according to my Garmin. Disney's mile markers would sometimes be a half mile too soon and sometimes they were a half mile too late. I'm pretty sure that's why Disney's chip time made it look like I was running too fast in the first 10K while my Garmin time was pretty solid. Disney had water and Gatorade stations every few miles. Sometimes they were 2 miles apart and sometimes they were 4 miles apart. I made sure to walk each and every aid station.

Animal Kingdom

All along I noticed runners stopping to get their pictures taken with Mickey Mouse and other Disney characters. Didn't they get the memo? Didn't they know this was a race? It was still dark on the long road from Magic Kingdom to Animal Kingdom. As we entered Animal Kingdom, it was getting light out and once again I noticed runners doing strange stuff. It looked like they were interested in getting in line for Expedition Everest during the race. Really? I snickered and kept going.

It was now light enough to see the construction on Avatar world at Animal Kingdom. I recognized it instantly from the "mountain" hanging in the sky that looked like a photograph of one of the floating mountains on the planet Pandora. I recognized it instantly as I ran and I knew that Disney was building an Avatar world without having to read it on some blog somewhere. I was still feeling good and my strategy of running a little fast but not too fast while walking at every water station seemed to be working. I was also beginning to pour water over my head at the water stations in addition to the water I was drinking. While I didn't feel uncomfortably hot, I was sweating and I was getting tired.

Disney Hollywood Studios

The Disney marathon course took us out of Animal Kingdom and headed toward Disney's ESPN Wide World of Sports. Since this wasn't a theme park area, they had us log a lot of miles in there. At one point we ran into a baseball stadium where a sizeable crowd was cheering us on. Disney really knows how to throw a party and they brought those skills to hosting this marathon. I thought we spent 19 miles in Wide World but I guess it was only 10K, still this brought us to the ¾ marathon point and we were about to enter Disney Hollywood studios. I kept checking the time and my pace was off. I wasn't going to BQ at this race and I wasn't even going to PR. The distance from Hollywood Studios to Epcot was astoundingly short. Unlike the distance from Magic Kingdom to Animal Kingdom, It seemed like Epcot was just across the street from Hollywood Studios.

Epcot

I was delighted as I entered Epcot and my body still wasn't sending the Bonk signal. But I knew I was tired. I mean really tired. Still I didn't feel like I had to walk. The heat and humidity had made a difference so I decided to relax, walk a little more, eat pretzels and stop for more photo ops. I was still perplexed by runners stopping to stand in line. The only photos I had stopped for were for characters where there was no line. I even stopped to snap a selfie across the lagoon from the Epcot ball at about mile 24. At about mile 25, it became apparent I wasn't going to be able to run faster even if I wanted to so if there was a wall in this race, I'd say I hit it at mile 25.

Partial Victory Again

Though I had not succeeded in making a BQ in January, securing my "right to goof off" for the rest of the 2016 running season, I had managed to push the wall out from the low 20-something miles to a LOT closer to 26.2 miles. My time was 4:07:33 which was only 3 minutes slower than my first marathon despite the fact the temperature and humidity were terrible for running. I began to wonder if I could get rid of the wall altogether. And I didn't reach the end of the Disney marathon wondering if I was crazy for having attempted a marathon in the first place. It didn't feel like it at the time, but I had made real progress.

The Disney medal is heavy. It is large, round, brass plated and VERY shiny. It has raised Mickey ears and it feels like something you would expect to get after 26.2 miles of running. I saw some people with 6 medals around their necks. Those were the crazies who had done the Dopey Challenge. They got 4 medals for actual races: the 5K, 10K, half and full marathons. Then they got a medal for the Goofy challenge which is half and full and they got a sixth medal for the Dopey Challenge which is all 4 races. It costs over $600 to register for the Dopey challenge. A marathon might be worth $150+ but I couldn't imagine myself paying that kind of money to run a 5K or even a 10K!

Massage

After the race, I decided to take advantage of the VIP treatment I signed up, and paid extra for. I had an all you can eat brunch in a special tent. There were eggs and sausage and lots of fruit. Best of all there was an area where I could get a massage for $10. I paid for the massage using cash I'd brought on the run just for this purpose. It was one of the best decisions I ever made. After Disney I had a lot of muscle lumps. This was fatigue soreness and not chronic pain but it felt good to have a massage therapist find and intervene in all those sore "lumps" that had built up over the marathon. After I ate I headed back to my room to shower and change. I tried to take an ice bath but got the water too warm in the tub so it was only slightly cooler than room temperature. I noticed one toe was bleeding. A little. Not bad for 26.2 miles to have one teeny weeny little ooze of blood from one toe. After all I was wearing the T7 which is Brook's minimalist racing flat! After my shower I went to Downtown Disney to have my medal engraved and to get a steak dinner at House of Blues. I'd been eating mostly vegetarian and fish during training but I had planned to eat like a king after my marathon and I certainly did!

Feeling Better

When I reflect on how I felt after Disney, I didn't feel nearly as sore or tired as I felt after Freep, but I was tired and I still needed a lot of rest. There is no way I would describe what I was feeling as "normal." When I ran a 5K or 10K and sometimes even a particularly easy half marathon, I would often yawn and say to myself, "That was fun now let's go do something else!" This was not the way I felt after Disney. I knew I'd put my body through something difficult and I knew I needed to rest. Even with the massage immediately after the race, though soreness was not much of an issue, I was still in disbelief that it was possible to feel anything like "normal" after a race of this distance. If a more experienced runner had said to me they felt like they had just finished a 5K I would assume they were joking with me or bragging. I didn't know what I didn't know.

My time was 4:07:31 which was only 3 minutes slower than my performance at Freep, despite being warm and quite humid. And of course this was still not fast enough to qualify me for Boston so my plan to just "goof off" and simply "run for fun" in 2016 would have to wait. For a while, I briefly considered a "marathon a month" plan but my coach talked me out of it as it would be putting too much stress on my body. Those following the Hansons method are advised to never do more than 3 marathons in 2 years and I had done 2 marathons in less than 3 months.

Training for Mountains to Beach

My First True Full Round of Marathon Training

Now that Disney was behind me, and I had been talked out of my marathon a month idea, I started looking for a new marathon for my next BQ attempt. I had set up my own training schedule for Disney that was simply a clone of what I had done for Detroit. I still relied on my coach's comments on my runs but I didn't ask her to tweak the schedule in any way. I had also added on distance and I had run during some pretty awful weather. By adding miles on easy days, I did some weeks approaching 80 miles getting ready for Disney. We had enjoyed a relatively warm winter so far, but now the ugly was just ramping up and I wanted to avoid running on ice and I especially wanted to avoid running in the dark. I searched for Marathons to try to BQ and one that stood out was a downhill affair called Mountains to Beach. It meant flying to California around Memorial Day to run but I'd already had to fly to Disney for a race so I decided to go for it. The most attractive feature of M2B was the 32 percent Boston qualifier ratio. For a race that didn't insist you were within so many minutes of your BQ time just to sign up, they had an incredibly high ratio of runners that actually qualified. I signed up right away. There was no way I was going to walk around "thinking about it" until the race sold out. I'd made that mistake during the summer of 2015 and missed the chance to participate in several good races that sold out quickly including the Color Run 5K.

I asked my coach to load a running schedule for me to prepare for Mountains to Beach. I also asked for reduced miles. I didn't want any more 70+ mile peak weeks, especially during the uglier part of the winter even if it was relatively mild. My 15 week marathon prep schedule would begin in earnest on

February 9th and my "down time" after Disney would end just a week or two before that date. This would be the first full marathon I knew about enough in advance that I could go through an entire Hansons marathon prep cycle. Hansons recommends we follow a 3 marathons in 2 years rule. This would be my third marathon in 12 months so any marathon after M2B would require careful consideration. At least this time I'd get the benefit of the full prep schedule. No more grafting in the last 8 or so weeks of a schedule designed to be done over twice that amount of time. I was optimistic about my chances to BQ at M2B and I couldn't wait to get started. Well, actually I could. I was tired of running in the winter. I was tired of running in the dark. I caught myself looking longingly at Zillow ads for property in Orlando so I could become a "snowbird" and do my prep down there but I didn't think my employer would accept 1,000 miles away as a suitable "work from home" arrangement! I do wish they would, though.

In the dead of winter, there aren't a lot of local races so I signed up for the Publix Florida Half Marathon. Three of us had planned to drive down together but those plans unraveled. I planned to fly or drive down myself and run it a week or two after Disney but when the time came I wasn't feeling well and I didn't go even though I had paid for the race. I asked Joyce to pick up my packet for me and I skipped the run. This was the most expensive Did Not Start of my running career. It was an expensive lesson not to sign up for "travel" races without thinking everything through. I didn't want another race entry fee to become a donation! Another thing I resolved was to do literally what was prescribed in the training plan. Nothing more. No addons. I might pick up a mile or two due to rounding errors. The Hansons method allows you to add miles on easy days and I'd added a lot of miles during my Disney prep. I would not make this a habit in the future. Maybe I'd sign up for a 10K (6.2 miles) instead of doing 6.0 called for on my schedule miles but no more piling on miles every other day assuming it was all good. Disney had shown me that simply adding quantity of miles was not enough to guarantee a BQ. This may have been because the added miles were ineffective and it may have been because the conditions at Disney were so hot. The bottom line is adding miles every day steals time away from other parts of life and adds stress in other areas. It's not worth doing if it doesn't guarantee a result and in running marathons nothing is guaranteed.

Seoul

I went on another business trip to Seoul in February, just after running embargo after Disney was lifted and I was starting preparation for M2B in earnest. It was a 14 hour flight and I had a strategy for getting on the right time zone. First of all, I would eat when they ate, not when I was hungry. Secondly I would sleep when it was dark out, not when I was tired. And, I would make sure I was tired at night by running. I had enjoyed running so much on my previous trip to Korea, I decided this time I would do even more.

Puff the Magic Dragon

I got up the Sunday morning after my flight and headed out of my hotel toward the Han river for a planned half marathon practice run. This was going to take place after only a few hours of "airplane sleep" followed by a somewhat restful first night in my hotel trying to fight the urge to stay on US Eastern time. When I got to the river, imagine my surprise when I saw people with bibs running a full marathon! "Oh great!" I thought to myself, "I'll run with these guys!". The 3:45 pacer came along. Actually there were two of them. There were front and back 3:45 pacers so I stayed between them. Everybody else had already run 30km. I had just run a few km from my hotel. It was like shooting fish in a barrel! I cruised along with these guys all the way to their finish line, smiling all the way. They went across their timing mats and I went around them, took a quick selfie by their finish line then started the second half of my planned half marathon. That's when I met him. That's when I met Puff the Magic Dragon...

It turns out I had been running with a tail wind which now became a brisk head wind. It turns out running a brisk pace with jet lag is a very VERY bad idea. I was breathing hard and I wound up walking quite a bit. The hard breathing, when I'm are no longer able to carry a conversation, is a danger sign that indicates risk of an impending Bonk.

There are different types of leg muscles used for running. The first type, typical in older runners is called "slow twitch". These muscles can use oxygen and burn fat and are involved when running a slow to moderate pace. The second type, typical in younger runners is called "fast twitch". They are particularly good at high effort high speed running but they tire quickly. These fast-twitch muscles have two sub-types. For now I'll call them A and B. Fast twitch A muscles can use oxygen and fat much like slow twitch muscles. Fast twitch B muscles rely entirely on glycogen stores and are only good for a quick sprint. Once that sprint is over, a runner is "rewarded" with lactic acid which is the substance responsible for muscle pain and soreness. There are training runs referred to as Lactaid threshold runs. These are runs designed to be done at a pace slightly slower than the pace that would wake up the Fast twitch B muscles and release lactic acid. A runner who avoids "waking up" their fast twitch B muscles can go indefinitely, provided they drink liquids during the run, but once those fast twitch B muscles wake up, raid the glycogen cupboard and release lactic acid, the runner is pretty much finished for the day. Luke Humphery described it like this,

> "Depending on fitness level, some runners can go an hour at a modest pace before they begin to recruit the fast twitch fibers; others can go up to two. It is likely you'll rely on type I fibers exclusively during the first half or so of the marathon. As those fibers tire, the body will begin to employ the type IIa fibers, those slightly larger aerobic fast-twitch fibers. If you have trained properly, you will have enough leeway to get through the rest of the marathon using these fibers. … Issues arise when the undertrained runner is forced to go to the third line of defense; type IIb fibers. If you are relying on those fibers to get you to the finish line, things will not end well."

From experience, I would say **things will not end well** is a bit of an understatement. I've seen those videos of people either limping across the finish line or being carted off to the medical tent shortly after or sometimes even during the marathon. Some of them drank too much water. Yes that's a thing. If you feel water sloshing around in your belly during the run, skip some water stations!

Some of them drank too little and were dehydrated. If you have dry mouth, by all means drink at the very next water station even if it means losing some time. But quite a few of those folks you see in distress managed to wake up that third muscle group and for them "things did not end well." This is one of the promises that the Hansons method makes, that if you train properly you can get through a marathon without falling back on that least desirable set of muscle fibers.

The hard breathing involved in running at too fast of pace is what I call the breath of Puff the Magic Dragon. Watch out! When you hear him (in your) breathing, you might be 500 meters or less from the end of your ability to run. In fact, I'll go a bit further and say if you hear Puff in the breathing of the runners around you, become mindful of your own breathing. It is quite possible you are being "sucked along" by a group running too fast for present conditions! Once that third muscle group wakes up, you might be 20 miles distance from the end of your marathon, but you are actually 500 meters from the end of your ability to run your intended pace. As I returned to my hotel alternating running and walking and thankful for the Seoul traffic that caused me to wait at half a dozen intersections, I thought to myself "No big deal, I'll do better tomorrow!" And I did.

I found running tracks almost everywhere in Seoul. They were next to the river, they were in parks but the best one of all was a heavily padded 1.5 mile loop in a park about a half mile from the National Assembly. I ran all these trails while I was over there. As an inexperienced runner, I couldn't perceive the stress I'd caused myself by running too aggressively with jet lag on that first day but I found out soon enough.

Race

Just as I was beginning my formal preparation for M2B, Hansons announced a special screening of the film Race at a local theater. Race was the Jesse Owens story and it was inspirational. The Olympics were being held in 1936 in Nazi Germany which was a regime where they would have preferred to ignore someone's achievements based on their perceived "race" or the color of their skin. Jesse went on to win multiple gold medals in spite of the conditions and even though some people both in Nazi Germany and even back at home in the US refused to give Jesse proper respect and recognition at the time, his records were something nobody could take away from him.

To me this reinforced the egalitarianism of running. For me, the fact that Hansons was hosting a screening of the film helped to highlight the egalitarian nature of their running program. Their program was open to athletes of all ages, backgrounds and abilities. For the past three Olympics, Hansons has had one of their athletes on the US Olympic marathon team. Yet Hansons group runs are targeted at community members who just happen to enjoy running, regardless of pace or ability.

As I prepared for M2B, I reflected on how lucky I was to have such an excellent community to support me. When I think about Daniels' assertion that coaching is relatively unimportant compared to other factors, I have to disagree because without proper coaching, I might have had to learn some lessons through time lost from racing due to injury or burnout.

The screening of the film Race occurred on the day I landed coming home from Korea. I knew I wouldn't sleep much on the plane but I still wanted to go. I was glad I went to the screening and there was strong turnout from the Hansons running community. Of course not getting enough rest is another factor that can contribute to burnout and this, along with my foolish decision to push too hard running over in Korea would soon provide a timely lesson for me.

Burnout

Physical Burnout

I remembered running in deep snow in November, but by March I was just plain sick of all aspects of winter running, from the time it took to put layers on top of layers, to doing running laundry every few days, to that doggone Garmin heart rate bra strap thing, to the slippery conditions that dictated thinking hard about every single footfall. I had been running my new schedule for a few weeks. I was running marathon pace for my long runs and tempo runs. This is what I thought I was supposed to do but I was tired. I was very tired. And there were more and more days I simply didn't feel like running. I was hitting a training wall. And my little encounter with Puff in Korea had been a nail in the coffin. My body was shutting down and I was meeting Puff at mile zero point five of ten mile runs all of a sudden! I was running a lot less than I had been running at the peak of my running before Disney but I was not liking it one bit.

There were a couple of times I was scheduled for long runs that I simply blew them off. There was one day when I had a migraine and was so sick I never even tried to get out of bed. I attributed the lost day due to illness to a 24 hour bug but even after I felt better, I wasn't "into" running any more. I emailed my coach and asked what was going on. I also started researching runners' burnout. While my 24 hour bug explained one of my down days, it didn't explain the pattern of shortening runs drastically or skipping them altogether.

Slowing Down

Katie replied with something I already knew but had forgotten, that first and foremost running should be fun and she didn't mind if I shortened or skipped running days on my schedule until I was feeling better. I had a nagging suspicion that I might be pushing too hard so I asked her to remind me once more what paces I should be running. Her reply was a huge eye opener.

I had somehow missed or perhaps ignored these training paces before. All along I had been racing to train. I had been doing better in my practice runs and arriving at races so tired I just got by. Coach Katie wrote,

> "If you lost these training paces (for 3:55 marathon), here they are again:
> Recovery jog: super easy, no specific time
> Easy Runs (1-2Pace) : 9:58 – 11:18 min/mile
> Moderate Easy Run / Long Run: 9:38 – 11:18 min/mile
> Marathon Pace Run/ Tempo Run: 8:58 min/mile
> Strength Run: 8:42 min/mile
> Speed 5k-10k Pace: 7:50 – 8:10 min/mile"

My goal was just under 9 minutes a mile. And the only time I should be running that pace was during my tempo runs. The only time I should be going any faster was during the speed or strength portions of my intervals. Furthermore, my long runs should happen at 0:30 to 1:30 SLOWER than my marathon goal pace. And my easy runs should be 0:30 SLOWER than the long runs. I was pushing WAY too hard on all of my runs and only a few weeks into preparation for M2B, it seemed that no matter how hard I tried, I couldn't consistently run my marathon pace. And my breathing was way out of control. For me there was no carrying on a conversation running at any pace.

There are two thresholds involved in running. One is the Aerobic threshold. This is the point where the body is working hard but not too hard. This is the zone doctors want everyone to do about half an hour a day several days a week for good cardiovascular health. Running slower than aerobic threshold is called easy or recovery running. Running faster is called long or tempo running. It should be possible to carry on a conversation when running slower than aerobic threshold without any difficulty at all. It should be possible to carry on a conversation above aerobic threshold with minor difficulty. When tempo runs or long runs are being done too fast, the body never makes the adaptations required for long distance running.

The other threshold is called the Anaerobic threshold. This is the point where the body is working so hard, it can't sustain the effort for very long. This pace is accompanied by hard breathing and it is very difficult to carry on a conversation while running at this speed. This type of running typically done in interval training. If tempo run paces cross the anaerobic threshold, you get a good workout but you don't necessarily become a better endurance runner. If interval work for speed or strength fails to exceed the anaerobic threshold, you don't get the benefits of those workouts either.

I had been spending too much time at or above the second threshold and it meant I wasn't getting the full benefit of all the training I was doing. By slowing down, my body could gradually make adaptations and my level of fatigue reduced enough I felt like "I got my life back." I was paying for coaching but on the topic of pace, I hadn't been exactly "coachable." I'm so glad I finally listened to my coach and slowed down my practice runs!

Injury Avoidance

I sat down and talked with one of Hansons' elite athletes, Dani Miller. She had just run Olympic trials and had come back with an injury. She was devastated that she was unable to run and I could hear it in her voice. It turns out she had run in Los Angeles with stress fractures. The 2016 Olympic trials course consisted of a roughly 6 mile loop the athletes would complete multiple times. Dani's coach told her she could stop at mile 8 if she wanted to. She kept going. He reminded her each time she passed but she kept going. She finished the entire marathon and pushed through her pain and it had cost her a 6 week running embargo.

I took what Dani said to heart and listened to my body. I ran only when I felt like running. I ran only as far as I felt like running and I slowed the heck down. I also tossed that BQ goal out the window. I was two for two hitting walls in marathons. Sure I'd managed to push the wall further out in my second marathon but my time was 3 minutes slower. The only way I was going to be able to enjoy running was if I simply did it for enjoyment and stopped worrying so much about the clock. And I resolved to train to race rather than race to train. No more PRs at group runs and practice races. I would save my best efforts for when I was on the clock in a race I had trained for.

I was still pretty skeptical that running slower for my long runs would help my body remember how to run at my marathon pace but I finally gave in and ran exactly what my coach prescribed. I did this for each and every run from then on. No more childish fantasy that running faster would somehow make me miraculously run a marathon in under 3 hours when I was having serious trouble breaking 4. I would focus on breaking 4 hours with no miracle required and if I didn't make it due to hot weather, a cold, a long trip to the bathroom during the race or some other factor beyond my control, I wasn't going to let it ruin my run!

After about a week, I was back up to my normal training volume but there was no longer constant fatigue because I was running everything at proper pace rather than too aggressively. I was not caring about speed so much. Well, actually I was glancing at my wrist more to check if I needed to slow down. Up until now I'd been catching myself dragging when I was tired and kicking in more Jeff to make a certain pace. I began to appreciate the value of banking Jeff instead of banking time. Time is a check that my body will almost always bounce. But if I bank endurance by running slower during training and even during the actual marathon, my body can afford to cash the 10K check that comes due after the 20 mile jog in a marathon. I knew all of this in my head, but I had never actually lived it at marathon distance.

Mental Burnout

A lot of my running was done in the dark. I had a light that snapped on my shoe. I had a lighted armband and I had a headlight. My headlight had a bright LED as well as a red light. I preferred red because it didn't mess with my night vision. And still the drivers on 14 mile tried repeatedly to take me out as they frantically made their turns into Biggby coffee. I had to find a way to run more miles in daylight. I had a couple pairs of gore tex running shoes and I was putting a LOT of miles on them. I would wear the GTXs whenever it was snowing, raining or slushy. This was almost every run. REI loved me. I bought so many base layers and other cold weather tech there I think REI named a wing of the store after me. I should also mention that I was one of the best customers at Hansons Running in 2015.

During that year I went from running in Rockport walking shoes to owning as many as a dozen pairs of proper running shoes. Whenever Hansons brought in a shoe company for demos, I'd try the shoes and more often than not, I'd buy a pair. Having a variety of shoes can help prevent burnout but I had been running too fast and I had to have a wakeup call from my coach to refocus. This one instance where paying for coaching was worth it. In Jack Daniels' book, he refers to four factors that determine success for a runner. Ability, motivation and opportunity are three and direction or coaching is a smaller factor by comparison to those three. As I was mentally committed, had a reasonable ability and plenty of opportunity to run, coaching was an important factor to get me from dabbling in running to making serious BQ attempts in less than one year.

I could compare my positive running experience to the experience of the author Helen Macdonald in "H is for Hawk." She compares her experience in training a Goshawk to that of the writer TH White in his book "Goshawk". While White wasted time reinforcing negative behaviors in his hawk, Helen enjoyed more success because she invested time doing research beforehand and enlisted the help of experts when she had questions. While White had self-sabotaged, she was honestly motivated to succeed. I did not get into running after years of research but I hired someone who had done this research and she guided me around many of the pitfalls I might otherwise have fallen into. I spoke to so many runners who suffered knee, hip, back and other discomforts or who were sidelined for weeks with stress fractures. I made it a point to reach out to my coach with questions whenever a new hairbrained running scheme entered my brain or an unexpected ache or pain cropped up.

One such scheme was my "Marathon a Month" idea that would have been a great fiasco if I had undertaken such a thing at that point in my training. I mentioned a no pain mantra but I never really minded soreness after a good strong run. But I never liked starting a run still sore from the day before. To me, starting runs sore day in and day out was a recipe to lose motivation and stop running.   One key was slowing down recovery runs and another was doing all my runs at the correct, instead of way too fast of a pace. Look into the Hansons coaching plan if you want the benefit of a coach you can ask questions by email and get prompt responses. At this time they call it the silver level coaching plan. This plan worked very well for me and I highly recommend it.

It was advice from my coach as well as that of other runners that helped me cope with the mental burnout associated with running in the dark on slippery conditions. It also helped me avoid physical injury that might have resulted if I had simply tried to "push through" those times when I didn't "feel like" running.

Drahner Loop

Double Drahner

Of all the Hansons group runs, my favorite is the Sunday morning Lake Orion run over the Seven Sisters. I had run this several times before during my Disney prep but during my M2B prep I decided to take it to a different level. I planned to never miss Sunday morning runs. This meant going to church Saturday evening because my Sunday mornings were spoken for. This meant passing up invitations for any number of alternative activities. I had running buddies repeatedly try to talk me out of running Lake Orion. Either it was too cold. Or too icy. Or too wet. Or too hilly. Baaahhh! to all their distractions. Lake Orion was my goldilocks zone.

Every now and then I'd noticed elite runners passing me because they had "added on" doing the Drahner loop. One day I worked up the courage to take the left off of Indian Lake Road onto Barr Road and see what the Drahner loop had to offer. After running Drahner, the Seven Sisters felt more like speed bumps. They are steep speed bumps but speed bumps nonetheless. Drahner wasn't any steeper but it was a whole lot longer. It seemed that once you made that right onto Drahner from Barr, you were running pretty much the next entire mile uphill. After you pass the Lutheran retreat house on the left, you reach the Benedictine Monastery on the right. This is just before a steep downhill and you know the hill is over. Whew! There are a couple more hills before you rejoin the Seven Sisters loop, but you have run past the highest point in Oakland County so the worst is over.

One thing I really liked about the M2B prep schedule coach Katie provided was that now there were multiple 18 mile long runs on Sundays. I had specifically asked her about doing longer long runs. I remember reading that it would be OK to do longer runs if I could finish my workouts in under 3 hours. My previous "short changed" prep cycle long runs maxed out at 16 miles. Better still, I now had 4 18 mile runs in a row in my schedule. Two of the 18 mile runs were 4 mile warmups, followed by 10 mile tempos and then 4 mile cooldowns. Two were simply 18 mile long runs. I'm so glad I figured out the proper pacing before tackling those long runs!

It turns out if you run the Drahner loop twice, you get 19 miles. I had a prescription for 18 so I ran Drahner twice and walked the last mile back to the running store. The first week I did this I felt certain I had run a whole marathon. As I got back to Conklin road, I was tired and thirsty. I had decided to mix Ucan and bring it on the run but I hadn't brought extra water. There is a party store at Conklin and Miller that opens Sunday mornings at 11 so I went in to pick up a bottle of water. They wanted 3 bucks for a bottle of smart water. Then the guy didn't want to take my debit card. Really? I don't carry extra "stuff" when I run. I carry my insurance card, ID and one debit card. I asked him if he really intended to send away a thirsty man who had just run 18 miles simply to avoid paying bank fees on a $3 transaction. He sold me the water. That party store owner wasn't the only person to seem annoyed with us runners.

There are between 10 and 30 of us who regularly come into Lake Orion on Sunday mornings at 8am, park near Hansons store and proceed to run between 9 and 21 miles. Many of us then spend money in Lake Orion. One week a local guy joined us for the run. He lives about a mile south of our running loop on Conklin road. He had run several marathons and came to run with us mostly out of curiosity. He let me know that sometimes the locals get annoyed with us running on the dirt roads and slowing down traffic. He pointed out the house of a local man who is over 100 years old as we ran along Conklin road. It was nice running with a local tour guide!

While most drivers smile and wave, I've seen some scowls from a handful of cars that pass us so it didn't catch me completely off guard when he mentioned hearing some complaints about runners. He also mentioned bikes that sometimes ride 4 abreast on narrow, hilly roads so that cars would have nowhere to go to avoid them. He was saying it would only be a matter of time before one of those bikers got hurt. I've noticed this during the Royal Oak runs as well. Especially at the Royal Oak runs because we run in the evenings and sometimes we narrowly avoid cars that simply don't see us or are in too big of a hurry to look for pedestrians.

My second DD week was much better and by the third week I was getting *comfortable* with doing 18 miles that included almost 500 feet of vertical climb to the highest point in Oakland county, *twice*. Everybody thought I was crazy and even the elite runners would look at me and shake their heads! At my pace, doing 18 miles was a 3 hour affair. The elites could come in and do what was for them an easy-paced 20 mile run and be gone an hour before I was done. I had a chance to meet two time US Olympian Desiree Linden at one of these Sunday morning runs. I was actually running with her and the rest of the elites for almost a whole mile which must have been some kind of warmup for them because after that mile they pulled away and disappeared over the hills ahead of me. I wouldn't see them again because they were doing the normal seven sisters loop and I was doing Drahner. Every now and then one of the Elites who had started later than me but was running faster than me would overtake me on Drahner but for the most part I ran alone.

One thing I noticed running Drahner is I was feeling better and stronger and I was confident that all those hills were helping to increase my strength and stamina. It was like combining intervals with long runs. Desi and some of the other elite runners used other loops to add on to the Seven Sisters. You could make a half marathon out of this run if you wanted to, always including Predmore, Harmon and Miller roads which contained some of the steepest hills. Drahner was more of a gentle slope but it went on and on and on. As you turned left from Indian Lake Road onto Barr, you encountered what was actually one of the steepest parts of the Drahner loop. Then you got to go down a bit but mostly up. That was the story of the Drahner loop. It was mostly up and it never seemed to end. One day my coach told me she would never do Drahner for a recovery run. I understood why.

My third and last DD week was by far my best experience. By now my legs were itching to do ups and downs over 18 miles followed by a nice recovery walk. It turns out the walk was just as important as the hill work because I was never sore after these runs. I had a wonderful experience for this last run because it was nice and cool. Well actually I should say cold. It was actually snowing! There was a half an inch or so of accumulated snow along the roads as I arrived in Lake Orion that morning and as I got past the Benedictine

Monastery on Drahner road approaching Lake George road I actually saw snow flurries! I'll take snow flurries over heat any day. My friends had opted for a different location this week because one thing runners really try to avoid is slippery conditions when the weather is around freezing. The seven sisters can get pretty treacherous when the weather is close to freezing and a snowfall from several weeks ago can still pose a problem with icy patches and muddy patches the day of your run. I was blessed that conditions were relatively dry and I had no trouble finding good footing. I could focus on churning out the miles and this time as I reached mile 18, I didn't bother to even glance at that party store. I walked into town and went to breakfast at CJ's.

I would enjoy a veggie omelet at CJs after a run. If I felt particularly hungry, I'd add a side of sausage patties. I'm a vegetarian of convenience. I don't mind eating meat now and then but I tend to avoid it. I knew this would be my last visit to Lake Orion for a while because I had signed up for the OneAmerica Mini Marathon in Indianapolis and that's where I would be running my next 18 mile long run.

Indy Mini

The Indy Mini is the largest half marathon in the United States. In the final weeks leading up to the Indianapolis 500, the city of Indianapolis hosts a half marathon which includes one lap of the famous "Brickyard." One of the resources I use to help my running is YouTube. Hansons has a lot of good videos on YouTube. Another series that caught my eye was about an Ethiopian born American runner named Meb Keflezighi. I've watched so many of his videos but my favorite was the one he called "my last marathon." Of course it wasn't his last marathon but it showed even an Olympian like Meb can have a bad day and he shared some important lessons he learned that day in that video.

I was at breakfast at CJs after one of my Lake Orion runs and one of the other runners mentioned that Meb was going to run Indy mini, and that he was going to start in the back so he could run "with" us. I got on my smartphone, found the race, signed up and paid before leaving the breakfast table. I looked forward to seeing and running with Meb and I hoped that if I was lucky, maybe I'd even get a photo with him!

Hotel at the Start Line

I made reservations at a hotel right next to the start line of the race. It was pricey but I was only there for one night as I planned to drive home after the race. I wasn't looking forward to 5 hours of driving after an 18 mile run so "plan A" was for me to treat Indy mini as an easy run and go to Lake Orion to do DD the next day.

I took off early from work so I could drive down and get checked in to my hotel and get to the Expo at a time Meb was likely to still be there. Not only did I make it at the right time, I actually got in the line to see Meb just as he arrived. I didn't dare leave his line.

The Expo

One of my favorite quotes is from Meb after Olympic trials in Los Angeles this past February. There was another member of the US team, Galen Rupp, on Meb's heels interfering with Meb's pace. When asked about what he said to the guy, Meb smiled and said, "It wasn't a particularly friendly conversation." Meb added, "I told him the road is open! It is not a track!" So when I got to the front of the line to see Meb, I said to him "The road is open". He broke out in a huge smile and as I started to leave he looked up and said to me, "The road is open!"

I was geeked for the Indy Mini race and the odds that I'd run it easy and do DD on Sunday were rapidly diminishing. One issue was rain. I really hadn't had to run in the rain much and storms had been predicted for the day of the race but the forecast was changing and the storms were no longer expected during the race. If it was sloppy or miserable out there, I'd revert to my plan to drive home and do my long run Sunday. But if it was nice, I'd find a way to add on 5 miles, get my 18 out of the way at Indy and do a nice easy run Sunday instead of Saturday.

After the Expo, I decided to go find a route to do my add-on five miles. I ran from my hotel, the Courtyard Marriott across the river and into the neighborhoods on the other side. As long as there was either sidewalk to run on or paved streets without heavy traffic, I was happy. I even fantasized about inviting Meb to accompany me on the same route after tomorrow's run. Yeah, I have quite the imagination! I got 8 miles in, including a nice run through a state park and several miles along rather ordinary looking urban streets. It was hot and I found it hard to believe that I was running in snow flurries doing DD just a week ago! That evening I planned to go to sleep early but that plan was foiled by Indianapolis' minor league baseball team. They had a game going at a stadium just outside my window and when they let fireworks off at the end of the game, there was no way I was sleeping through that commotion. I didn't get as much sleep as I had wanted but I rested well.

The Race

I got up the morning of the race and headed to the lobby looking for breakfast. I didn't bother mixing up any Ucan as I still wasn't sure if conditions warranted doing 18 miles today and even if they did, I figured I could "live off of the course". This is runners' slang for making do with the stuff they hand out during a race rather than lugging snacks and your own liquids. I found a nice yogurt parfait and wolfed that down along with some overripe bananas the hotel had put out for runners to enjoy for free. It was crowded. I mean crowded. I'd run two marathons and a bunch of half marathons and by comparison this race was big. Incredibly big. I heard on the news they were expecting more than 30,000 runners. I heard from several people that the race sometimes draws as many as 55,000 people. I believed it. As I came outside, I saw that I was about 15 feet from the start line and I would have to walk a half a block to get to my start corral for wave 2.

But the start corrals were already full as they were starting a 5K ½ hour before the half marathon. If only I'd known about this, I'd have signed up for both. Once that race started, they let us into the corrals and I took the opportunity to have another runner snap my photo with the JW Marriott in the background. I'd never run in a race where there was a 20 story billboard at the start line...

There were several thousand runners in the wave in front of mine and there were a lot of waves behind me. This was a huge race! Frankly there was more hoopla surrounding this half marathon than there was for some marathons. It seemed like there were water stations every few hundred feet. I guess officially they were every mile but I could sometimes see two of them at a time along the course. There was an incredible level of crowd support. The Disney marathon, while it was a larger race in terms of athletes, had a lot less crowd support because it started so early in the morning. Indy mini started after dawn and there were crowds along almost the entire length of the 13.1 mile course.

Going for Sixteen

As I started out, I noticed the weather was fine and I made the decision to run my long run pace instead of my easy run pace. I started cranking out 9 minute miles from the start line at my hotel to the speedway at about mile 6. Just before we reached the entrance to the Indy 500 speedway, there was a group holding a sign with one my favorite bible verses. In fact it was the verse Fr. Cassidy shared with me at the time he first encouraged me to start running marathons...

I quickly snapped a photo of the group. I guessed by their brown vestments with plain rope cinctures that they were probably Franciscan friars.

Runners enter the speedway through a tunnel that goes underneath the track. The stands are huge and I couldn't imagine how many people it might take to fill them. I would later find out there are permanent seats for about 225,000 fans and that the total attendance on race day is often estimated to be over 300,000. The Indy 500 track is 2.5 miles. I calculated that if I ran the track 3 times instead of once, I'd make my 18 miles goal so I decided to ask the race marshals if they'd allow me to do an "extra" lap when I got to the end of the track. Whether I'd do a second "extra" lap was to be a game-time decision. I'd rather add on a couple more miles after the Indy mini than have my chip time make it appear I'd walked the whole thing.

One thing I became keenly aware of during Indy was the "flock effect." Ever watch a flock of birds and see them all turn in unison and fly different directions, sometimes several times in one minute? Running in a large race feels like I would think those birds feel. There's a certain sense of camaraderie that comes from going in the same direction at about the same speed as 50,000 other people and I enjoyed it immensely. Leaving the tunnel that goes under the track, we entered the pit area and approached the actual oval track. I'd always heard the thing was steeply banked but I didn't think it was banked much at all. I had expected a simple oval track like a high school quarter mile with two straight sections and two curved sections but this track was much larger. It was an oval but it had 4 straight sections and 4 curved sections and the banking was gentle on all sections of the track.

Double Indy Track Loop

As I approached the end of the track I saw race marshals guarding the spot where runners might go back onto the track for another lap. Of course nobody was doing it but I decided it didn't hurt to ask so I ran up and said, "If I don't care about my time, can I do another lap?" To my surprise the guy said "Go ahead!" so I ran another lap of the Indy 500 track! I approached a section where orange cones forced runners to run over timing mats and I purposely jumped over the cones to avoid having my chip read twice on the same mat. At the finish line there is a section of the original brick track that is left for posterity. A tradition for those running the Indy mini is to "kiss the bricks" and I decided it to do it on my first lap but I hadn't bothered getting a picture. This time around I took an opportunity to have someone snap a proper picture of me kissing the bricks. I wanted them to catch "The road is open" I had written on the back of my shirt so Meb could find me but that part of my shirt didn't make it into the photo.

As I completed the second lap, I realized I was no longer part of a flock. By taking a 2.5 mile detour, I had fallen back to a group of much slower runners and from now on, I'd be running a much faster pace than those around me if I simply continued running the pace I'd set from the beginning. It's a lot easier to run with a group than through it and this, along with the heat started to take its toll. When I reached the spot where I could have taken a third lap I decided I wouldn't bother trying to add on a third lap. Running back into downtown was easier and I knew the timed portion of the race was almost over as I saw my hotel coming up in the distance. I was stopping at almost every water station and eating all the goo I could find because I was doing 18 miles and I hadn't brought any Ucan on the run with me.

When I got to the end and got my medal, I noticed it was as heavy as a full marathon medal. I held it in my hand, quickly ate some snacks and headed out to put on another few miles. Downtown Indianapolis has canals below street level. They make for excellent running because there are no cars down there. They also can be a more humid place to run on a hot day and I was feeling it this day! I was so happy when I got to 18 miles and I walked back to my hotel for breakfast. I was a little worried that crossing the timing strips at the track twice would cause a problem but all seemed well as the system recorded my pace for the first 10K at about 9 minutes a mile and the rest of the half marathon at 11 minutes a mile. It made it appear that I had bonked when actually I had simply added on 2.5 extra miles on the Indy 500 track.

Breakfast

I had the breakfast buffet in the restaurant at the JW Marriott. There were actually three Marriott hotels in one largish building. There was a Courtyard, a Spring Hill Suites and the JW Marriott all joined by indoor corridors and meeting areas. At one point I glanced out the window and spotted a fourth Marriott outside. Somebody in Indy needs to develop some imagination when it comes to naming their downtown hotels! I mean 4 Marriott's all within sight of one another? Whose idea was this? I was able to charge my breakfast to my room even though my hotel was at the opposite end of the complex. The buffet was delicious. I had a made to order omelette loaded with veggies and cheeses. I had smoked salmon and capers and a huge pile of fruit. I also had a Belgian waffle loaded with another huge pile of fruit. This would put back a lot of the 1800 calories I'd just expended and would hold me for a good portion of my drive home.

Next Year: 26K!

I decided on the spot to sign up for the next year since signup was discounted the weekend of the race. This time I signed up for both the 5K and the half for a combined distance of 26K. This is really my favorite distance for a race and I looked forward to coming back to Indy next year to run such a fun half marathon with marathon-like crowd support. I hadn't seen Meb all day and it didn't surprise me that we couldn't find each other in a crowd of 50,000+ runners. I was so impressed at how he was so dedicated to inspiring people to run that he made time to come run indy with ordinary runners just a few months before he would run for the US in the 2016 Olympics in Rio.

The drive home was relatively uneventful and I wasn't hit with the same cramps I'd had driving down. If anything I expected them to be worse after such a long run but the drive was easier than I expected. The next morning I did an easy 9 mile loop of the seven sisters happy that my last 18-miler was now behind and my next really long run would be the Mountains to Beach marathon.

Mountains To Beach Marathon May 2016

Arrival in LA

At first, I reserved a hotel about 5 miles from all the action but after my experience at Indy mini, I knew it was worth paying extra for a hotel "right by the start/finish line" and that's what I did. I canceled my Holiday Inn reservation at Ventura Harbor and booked the Crowne Plaza which is the only hotel in Ventura Beach that has actual ocean frontage. In fact, the Crowne Plaza was right on the marathon route at about mile 25.5! Needless to say it cost about half again as much as the Holiday Inn would have cost. I also splurged on plane tickets. With the memory of my legs cramping during the drive down to Indy, I spent extra miles getting first class plane tickets. I didn't want to be crammed into a coach seat with sore legs. I also reserved a car for the trip. I have family in the LA area and when I made plans to see them the Friday I flew in, I decided to change my flight times so I would hit the LA freeways mid-day, well before "rush hour." Until I got there I had no idea how bad LA traffic can be!

My flight to LA was uneventful. I arrived at Detroit Metro airport early enough to have breakfast before boarding my flight. I then got on and they served us... breakfast again. I didn't mind because I wanted to be well fed and well rested for my run. When I got to LAX, I quickly found out why it's considered one of the worst airports in the country. The baggage claim area has low ceilings, poor visibility, feels claustrophobic, and seems tragically inefficient. I landed in terminal 5 but had to go through a tunnel to terminal 6 to claim my luggage. The monitors in terminal 5 simply displayed T6 for my flight's carousel number and I wasted some time wandering around looking for "carousel 6" before I noticed a short tunnel to terminal 6. Once I got my stuff, I went looking for the rental car shuttle. This was another study in inefficiency. There are 14 foot wide sidewalks outside the terminal between many lanes of busy traffic. Somebody decided there needed to be 13-½ foot diameter columns blocking these sidewalks so it would be necessary to walk in traffic get around each column and proceed to the rental car shuttle. Really? I didn't have to wait very long to board a Hertz bus but I did have to wait until they filled it to the point I thought people were going to start sitting on the roof. At the Hertz counter I had a half hour wait in a very very long line. I should have kept that free Hertz Gold club membership I had allowed to expire years ago.

To make up for the long wait, they offered me a larger Nissan Altima instead of the Chevy Spark I had reserved at no extra cost. The Altima had keyless ignition and one of those start/stop buttons so I didn't complain. Not digging for my keys every time I wanted to start the car was a big plus. This is something I'll want on the next car I buy. I hit LA traffic as I headed to see family in Murrieta, CA which is allegedly 1 hour from the airport. Yeah. Right. After a very painful 2 hour ordeal, I arrived at my cousin's house and we spent several hours visiting. I considered driving another few hours the rest of the way to San Diego to see more family but I realized this would mean the earliest I would get to my hotel would be 10pm Pacific time which is 1am my time. I decided it was best to try and catch them another time and I headed to my hotel n Ventura from Murrieta. Again the alleged distance is 2 hours but I spent close to 3 hours getting there.

Once I got my car parked and settled in my hotel I began to relax. The Crowne Plaza sits along the beach portion of the M2B marathon course and It's about ¾ mile from the expo and about ½ mile from the shuttle pickups for the marathon start. There are restaurants and shops in walking distance. Moving to this hotel from the Holiday Inn 5 miles further south was the best decision I ever made! I would not have to so much as look at a car the morning of my race. I needed a practice run so I went for a run from the hotel, proceeding south along the beach toward LA. The road left the beachfront and after about a half mile, I spotted a road going back down to the beach so I ran down. I was rewarded with a beautiful sunset! This would be the best sunset visible during my visit as there were no low clouds over the ocean to obscure the sun as it set. As I ran back toward my hotel, I ran out the Ventura boardwalk and back to finish out my planned distance.

Shakedown Run

Saturday morning I woke up at 3am which is around my normal wake up time of 6 in my home time zone. I didn't fight to get on the local time zone. One thing I dislike is getting up at 0 dark something for these marathons and I was going to use this timezone to my advantage. I was not planning to be dog tired and sleep deprived at the start line for this race! Another thing I dislike is the feeling I need to go do number two during a race. This was a real risk for me at M2B because my circadian rhythm has me going number 2 between 9am and noon at home. These 3 hours would be the first 3 hours of the marathon and I planned that

I would hit the bathroom well in advance of getting on the shuttle bus the morning of the race.

At 7am I wandered outside and there along the beach just outside my hotel there was a group of runners getting ready for a group run! I joined them. It turns out a local run club involved in M2B was sponsoring this morning's run! I ran 1.55 miles out with them then turned around and came back. This is my normal shakeout distance (5K) for the day before a marathon.

Yoga

As I ran with the group, I noticed an attractive young woman named Jessie setting up a popup yoga session next to the beach. I asked her if I could join and she said I was welcome to join and that donations were appreciated. After my 5K shakeout run I went to Yoga!

I needed the stretching and happily there were no airplane poses and only a limited amount of down dog. There were plenty of child's poses. At the end of the hour-long session I was feeling relaxed and ready for my marathon. My cousin David lives about 30 minutes from Ventura and he came over to join me for breakfast at my hotel after yoga. This was the David I ran with in Minnesota when I wasn't prepared and I'm sure he was having trouble believing his eyes that the old geezer who just about collapsed 30 years ago on a short run was about to do a full marathon tomorrow. We talked about family in California and and back in Michigan and about how everyone was doing. We had enjoyed a nice visit and when he headed back home, it was time for me to make my way to the expo.

Relaxation

There are quite a few running authors who will advise you to do almost nothing the day before a marathon. I'm one of them. One of the easiest of the many marathon pitfalls to avoid is failing to get adequate rest the day before the marathon! I went to the expo and picked up my bib, only spent about 45 minutes walking around and headed back to my hotel to goof off. The M2B expo was small compared to the expos at Disney or at Indy mini but it was still quite good. M2B is sponsored by Clif so the only snacks provided on the course would be Clif products and the bulk of those being handed out at the expo were Clif products as well. Clif makes a goo they call Clif Shots. They make an electrolyte replacement called Fluid. And of course they make Clif bars, yummy!

While at the expo, I met Ed and Linda as Ed was picking up his marathon bib. Ed is a triathlete and it turns out Ed and I run about the same pace. We decided to start the race together the next morning. Ed, Linda and I ate the pasta dinner which was a fundraiser for a local school. At $10 it was a good value and filling. We then went walking along the ocean after the pasta dinner. We saw the beginning of another beautiful sunset but a high cloud bank over the ocean obscured the sun before it could turn the color of orange I had seen the night before. This was a disappointment for Linda who like me, loves sunsets. Ed is jaded about sunsets because they live near Buffalo and can see them every day not far from their home. I've lived near the water several times in my life and I don't think I'll ever take sunsets for granted. Sometimes I get worked up over the color of the sky or the shape of a few clouds. Along the beach, I spotted a condo for sale for $795,000 for a mere 1,000 square feet. If I could have afforded to buy that place, I'm pretty sure I would never grow tired of watching the sunsets from Ventura beach! Though I'm quite sure I'd get sick of the LA traffic almost immediately.

Pace Team

I met two other people at the expo and they were our pacers Gabe and Hanook. Hanook would pace the 3:53 group for the first half marathon and Gabe would join us for the second half. Having a fresh pacer at the second half would pretty much guarantee us a rock-solid pace. Ed and I discussed strategy and we decided to hang between the 3:53 and 3:58 pace teams until mile 20. Then if we were feeling well we would make our move. This is something coach Katie had stressed. Come out slowly! **For every second you run faster than marathon pace at the beginning you might wind up adding a whole minute at the end!**

I set my alarm for 3am and tried to get some sleep but the nights before marathons are probably the least restful nights of sleep I ever get. I woke up and decided to eat a mere two Clif bars. Usually if I put something in, something comes out pretty quickly and my plan worked. I had a small bowel movement and I thought it would be enough to keep me out of the porta potties during the marathon. I don't mind stopping for number 1 but it's hard to run fast enough to make up for the time lost if you have to pay a visit to the porta potty for number 2 during a race. I mixed up two 8 ounce bottles of Ucan and put on the short sleeve M2B running shirt. Over that, I put on the long sleeve "Santa to Sea" running shirt I'd bought for $1 at the expo the night before. It turns out I had not packed any long sleeve running apparel! I assumed the weather in California would be as hot and sticky as it was in Detroit. In fact before I left that's what the forecast was calling for. It was supposed to be 60-ish degrees in the morning with 60% humidity and by the finish of the race it was supposed to be 70-

ish degrees and sunny. The reality was much different. It was in the low 50s the morning of the race and while it felt cold standing around, these were ideal running conditions.

Running Down to the Beach

The Shuttle

Ed was assigned the 4am shuttle but I caught the 5am shuttle so I could allegedly sleep more. Ed would see how he felt after 5 miles before he decided to stick with the sub 4 hour pace team or not. There were dozens of people walking to the shuttles and the lines were fairly long once we got there. There were porta potties next to the shuttle lines but very few people were bothering to use them.

You had to be careful because you could get on the wrong shuttle and ruin your whole day! There were half-marathon shuttles that would take you about halfway up to Ojai and there were full marathon shuttles that would take you to the correct start line for the full marathon. If you got on the wrong one, the race organizers made no official provisions to get you to the correct start line! As I got on the bus, the driver was asking each person getting on, "You're going to run the full, right?"

These were ordinary school buses which means they aren't designed for adult anatomy. My knees were sticking out in the aisle during our roughly half hour ride up to the start line. It was dark so I didn't really get much of an idea of the scenery as we were driving up to Ojai. I was confident I'd see everything I wanted to see as I ran down. I was not to be disappointed!

Starting in Ojai

I met Ed in Ojai and we hunkered down inside a US Post office. It turned out to be the only building open 24 hours in Ojai and it was about 20 feet from the start line. We took advantage of a warm place to wait out the time before the race. We talked and confirmed our pace planning. There were dozens of school buses required to shuttle us all up to Ojai from Ventura for the start but once we were there in the start corral, it wasn't as crowded as some of the larger races I'd run like Freep, Disney or Indy mini. By marathon standards, this race was modest sized.

I was cautiously optimistic about my ability to run whatever pace I wanted without getting bogged down behind walkers in narrow spots. I took a quick selfie of Ed and I in our start corral.

As we waited for the start I realized I wanted to visit the potty before the race so I wandered away looking for a shorter line. I didn't find one. When I returned to my corral, I didn't find Ed but I met Eugene who is a doctor finishing up his third year of residency in central California. He had driven down for the race. Eugene was interested in doing a sub 4 hour marathon so we decided to run together. I let him know I planned to avoid the 3:53 pacer like the plague until mile 20. I said at the time, "I don't even want to know what that guy looks like until mile 20!"

As they sang the national anthem, I had a different feeling at the start of this run than I had had before. I felt a kind of optimism. I picked this race because of the vertical profile. We would run 3 miles up gentle hills rising 300 feet or 100 feet per mile, then run 20 miles down gentle hills losing 1000 feet or 50 feet per mile. There was a 100 foot "bump" at the end then a little downhill to the finish along the beach. I felt rested and nothing on my body was sore or tense. For this race, I was in the third corral reserved for all those running 3:45 or slower. I purposely started at the front of the corral so I wouldn't be impeded by walkers or joggers. There was a bit of clothing debris at the start as people discarded cotton hoodies they wore to stay warm. I removed my long sleeve tech shirt and tied it around my waist. I wanted to keep it even though it had only cost a dollar because I liked the "Santa" artwork printed on the tech shirt. Having my bib on my shorts meant I could make clothing adjustments without fumbling with my bib. I swigged some Ucan at the start to stabilize my blood sugar and started my Garmin exactly as Eugene and I crossed the starting line timing mat.

Slight Uphill

The first 3 miles went pretty much as I expected. It was slow going because there was a slight uphill incline. This helped calmed down those jittery "faster, Faster, FASTER!" impulses that feel so good at the start of a marathon and can lead to bonking at the end. Our pace was around 9 minutes for the first few miles and I found the M2B organizers had set up water stations about every mile. I walked fast as I drank. It was better to stop or walk when drinking or eating than to choke and cough and wind up losing more time. In fact at the first water station I tried jogging while drinking and got a tiny bit down the wrong pipe. This was a good warning and reminded me not to try any drinking while running nonsense again for the rest of the marathon.

Often when I run I observe runners around me as my "canary in a coal mine". Yoga classes have taught me to listen to the breathing of those around me. When I hear wheezing and labored breathing around me during a run, I glance at my watch to check my pace. It's almost as reliable as having a pace alarm set on my watch! Sure enough, I caught myself speeding up even on the uphills. I was getting "sucked along" by groups of faster runners and Eugene was willing and eager to keep going. I reminded him of my desire to avoid learning what our pacer looked like before mile 20. At one point I spotted porta potties with no line around mile 6 and decided to take a quick pause. Of course my Garmin had auto-pause turned on so it was no longer showing chip time, for the rest of the race, my Garmin would be off by the amount of time I spent visiting the bathroom so I knew I would have to run just a tiny bit faster than my goal pace for my time to come out right at the end. I was hoping that by ducking in the bathroom, the 3:58 pacer would pass me and I'd be able to spend my time hanging closer to him until I was ready to make my move back to 3:53 well after the half.

Bathroom Break

I came out of the porta potty and saw a pacer in the distance but I couldn't quite read his sign. Thinking it was mister 3:58, I took off after him, gently but fast enough to gain on him by 100 feet every half mile. When I caught him, I realized I had been mistaken and I was now caught up with mister 3:53. Darn. And there was Eugene running a bit ahead of the pacer we had agreed to avoid until mile 20. Eugene saw me and fell back in with me. As we passed through beautiful orange groves around mile 9, we slowed our pace deliberately until the 3:53 pacer was once again about half a mile in front of us. I took my fourth swig of Ucan. I had taken one at the start, one at 5K and one at 10K. My plan was to drink it roughly every 5K with bigger gulps every 10K so that it would run out about mile 20. With water stations so frequent, I never had to worry about when to drink my Ucan. I knew I'd be able to chase it with water in 2 miles or less so I drank it whenever I felt like it.

This is an important consideration. You really should drink plain water along with any goo, Clif bars, Ucan or other "food-ish" nutrients. The Ucan claim to fame is it can stabilize one's blood sugar without waking up the digestive system because it is already in a state where the body senses it won't need to expend energy breaking it down. The last thing a runner needs during a marathon is for the body to steal blood from the legs and send it to the stomach to help digest something he has eaten during the run.

Living Off the Course

I also planned to live off the course. I'd had two 200-calorie Clif bars and I was expending about 3000 calories so I knew I needed some intake beyond the 200 calories of Ucan I had mixed up in my canteens. When the race organizers provided electrolyte fluid, I'd drink it. When they provided "goo", I'd eat it. We got our first Clif Shots just after the relief pacer Gabe joined us at the half marathon. I took a non-caffeine one and walked quickly while I ate it. I found that I was comfortable "speed walking" at the same pace as those running next to me so I didn't so much slow down as I changed my gait so I never "bounced" and never had 2 feet off the ground at once. This made it much easier to take my time, peel open the pouch and squeeze it into my mouth. I'm really not coordinated well enough to open packaging or eat or drink anything while running or even walking too fast.

One advantage to living off the course is weight. By not lugging along a lot of liquids and goos, I was saving weight. All I had to do was make sure I had used a variety of different supplement in practice races and I got used to living off the course in other races I'd run leading up to M2B such as eating the goo packets provided at RockCF and at Indy rather than insisting on bringing my own brand.

Second Half

At the half marathon point, the M2B course gets quite a bit steeper. It's an excellent opportunity to pick up pace without increasing effort. It's hard on the quads, though and I was grateful for the few rolling hills that came along. During the third quarter of the marathon, I could really feel my quads whenever we had an uphill stretch and I loved how it felt. The downhill of this race may not have been very steep but it was affecting my quads nonetheless. We were staying within ¼ mile of the 3:53 pacer now and sometimes we ran with him. I know this because I found my photo at about mile 17 and you can see me and the 3:53 sign in the same photo. Well at least we didn't pass the guy!

About mile 19, Eugene was itching to pick up the pace and pass the 3:53 pacer. I suggested we stick to our plan. I quoted Desi Linden, "**Trust the program**." In my head, I was looking at my watch and frantically doing math to figure out when I was "safe" to BQ even if I walked. At mile 20 I agreed we could now close half the distance to the pacer. We did this easily and at mile 22 we passed him and never saw him again. There was about a mile uphill at this point and even though it felt like we were running faster, what we were doing was not running slower. Almost everyone else was slowing down for the hill and a few runners were bonking and starting to walk slowly.

A Conservative Strong Finish

I was worried that I would get the dreaded "**Must. Stop. Now.**" signal at any moment and I really focused on running conservatively. I'd managed to run this whole marathon without poking that sleeping dragon called "glycogen stores" and I wasn't interested in waking him up until mile 25. We ran down the last little hill toward the beach and my hotel loomed large. This meant we were half a mile from the end and the bonk hotline still wasn't ringing. I was all smiles! I forgot that my watch had auto-paused and I thought I had another whole minute to spare but it didn't matter. At the pace we were running, I was comfortably below my Boston qualifying time of 3:55. As I passed mile 26, within smelling distance of the finish I saw Linda and she cheered me on. The fact she was still there implied Ed was somewhere behind me or she would have been with him in the finish chute. I said hello and smiled all the way to the finish line. **I had never finished a race this long feeling this good.**

We got to the finish and I asked Eugene if he wanted to keep going another 4 miles. My bonk signal had never gone off but I wanted to "trick" my body even more and get it used to the idea that a day's exertion was really 30 miles! I wanted to make sure I'd never again have to answer that phone call from my legs screaming "enough!" during a race.

Boston Gong!

We got our medals and started looking for a way to get out of the finish chute to take a recovery run along the beach but we kept finding interesting things to do. Like ringing the **BOSTON gong**! Yeah baby! I had finished this thing in 3:49 according to my auto-paused Garmin and when I checked my time on the official race web site they had 3:50:17 for my time which was still almost a 5 minute margin faster than I needed to go to Boston.

In my race photo, the finish clock is showing 3:47:13 and that would have been my time if I'd started at the back of my wave. There are usually two clocks visible as you approach the finish. One is "gun time" which is the time you would be running if you crossed the start mat at the very front of the first wave. The other is the time you would be running if you crossed the start mat at the very back of the last wave. You know your time is somewhere between these two times. It was a wonderful feeling running up to the finish line and seeing both clocks showing sub-3:55 times. In the photo, Eugene is next to me in orange, looking at the timing mat. I have "**two thumbs up**" in the

photo. Normally after 26.2 miles, lifting my thumbs is a thing I would have to struggle with!

The line for the Boston gong was a long one! The M2B race has one of the highest percentages of any race in the country, (roughly 32%) of runners who qualify to Boston . There are races with higher percentages (60%) but those races won't allow you to even register if you aren't already within 10 minutes of your BQ time. Eugene didn't make his BQ time but he met his goal of a sub 4 hour marathon. Eugene took my picture ringing the gong.

I didn't see Ed until later but I found out he ran quite a bit slower. It didn't matter to him, though. As a triathlete he would rather run marathons a bit slower anyway. There was a third runner I was with but I didn't notice her until later that afternoon. Allie had been shooting for 3:47 and she stuck with the 3:47 pacer. Until mile 24. She came in at 3:52. This is what can happen if a person pokes that glycogen dragon during a race. It consumes them during the last few miles and adds multiple minutes to their time. To go from 6 minutes ahead to 2 minutes behind us in only 2 miles, Allie had to do some serious walking. She was upset that she bonked but even with that bonk, M2B was a 30 minute PR for her!

After the Boston Gong, I ran down the ocean to take my ice bath. It was so cold all the surfers were wearing wetsuits. It felt wonderful. I then came back up and signed up for a complimentary massage. While I was waiting, Eugene and I got beers in the party area next to the finish chute. When it was time for my massage, Eugene said goodbye. He was going to meet some friends to go to Santa Barbara. I told him I might join him but I was content to sit around the beach all day and bask in my BQ! The M2B medal was somewhat lighter than other marathon medals but it was way nicer. It has a moving section with a mountain running scene on one side and a beach running scene on the opposite side. Way cool!

Rocket Toes

This marathon was a significant event for me. For the first time in my life I ran a great distance and came away from it feeling like I wasn't exhausted and feeling like I'd run a mere 5K. I haven't mentioned this before now but my running buddies Tammy, Joyce, Natasha, Terry and John had a nickname for me. It was "**Rocket Toes.**" I think they gave me that name because I was the fastest of our small but dedicated group of about half a dozen regulars who attended a lot of races and group runs together. But I never really felt comfortable with that nickname until today. Today I was quite at home with my friends jokingly calling me "Rocket-Toes."

Puff the Magic Dragon Sleeps Tonight

Compared to Seoul

I thought back to when I met Puff the Magic Dragon in Korea. I thought about how I hit that headwind heading back to my hotel from the finish line of their marathon and how pleased I was with myself for keeping pace with their 3:45 pace team! Knucklehead! In Seoul, not half a mile after I started breathing heavy I had started wanting to walk. A few hundred feet later I had started needing to walk. In an un-timed half-marathon practice run (with jet-lag)!

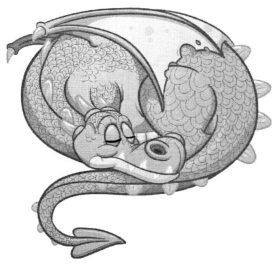

I've mentioned Puff before but it's time for me to say a little more about who this dragon is and why you never want him (awake) as your running buddy. You see Puff likes glycogen. He loves glycogen. He sleeps when you jog. As long as he slumbers, your slow twitch muscles cruise along using fat and oxygen to propel you at a moderate pace indefinitely. Lactic acid does not form while Puff is asleep and you finish your run feeling you've been on a pleasant (if brisk) walk.

Ultra runners and triathletes keep Puff asleep by carefully controlling their pace during their activities. But when Puff wakes up, you know it because you can no longer carry on a conversation with the runners around you. In moderate to warm weather, sweat starts to drip like somebody switched on a faucet. You start to hear yourself breathe. You start to really hear yourself breathe. You know you're done for when you feel hungry. You should never ever really feel hungry during a run. This isn't a time for digestion, it's a time for running. If your body is sending you messages about digestion, and stealing blood from your legs to send to your stomach to digest stuff even though you haven't eaten anything during your run, those signals are probably a result of Puff raiding your glycogen pantry! Puff is eager to send your ¼ mile worth of carb reserves so your muscles can handle the sprint you are running. Not running a sprint? Too bad. When those glycogen stores are gone, so are you!

Second Wind? Last Wind!

When Puff fully wakes up you feel a burst of energy! **Wow, NOW I CAN RUN!** That thing many runners call a "second wind" is more often Puff squandering the glycogen stores their fast twitch B muscles need for maximum performance. No, wait, make that normal performance. No, wait, make that any performance at all. It's fine if you feel that second wind the last few hundred meters as you approach the finish line. But if you feel that second wind when you have more than about a mile to go, Puff is about to breathe fire onto your legs, lungs, stomach, and brain and you are at risk of bonking. Quite often that second wind is really a runner's last wind!

At M2B, I managed to keep Puff asleep for 26.2 miles. I probably could have awakened Puff back when Eugene wanted to speed up at mile 24 but I remember choosing to run conservatively. I knew I could still make my BQ time and even if I walked so I simply stayed at my "sub anaerobic threshold" pace through to the end even though I probably could have safely exceeded it as I finished the last mile or so. It's funny. I felt that little hill at the end. I would have sworn we were speeding up. No. Everyone else was slowing way down. By keeping Puff asleep, I'd managed to save something for that little hill at the end.

Experienced marathoners can tell by conditions what pace they need to run to keep Puff asleep. Luckily for me it was a cool somewhat cloudy day on a downhill course. For an inexperienced marathoner like me, M2B was a very forgiving course. I might have awakened Puff back at mile 6 when I ran from the porta-potty to catch the 3:55 pacer having mistaken him for 3:58. I'm so glad that section was a little bit steeper downhill and Puff only yawned a little and went back to sleep.

On a warm day on rolling hills I might have had puff opening his eyes and not noticed it. This is one reason I don't run with music. I imagined listening to America's Ventura Highway as we ran into Ventura around mile 20. While I would have enjoyed hearing the song in real life, I was happy I could focus on the messages my body was sending. As I run more marathons and in more varied conditions maybe I'll get better at hearing Puff's initial stirrings but for now I must rely on the canary in the coal mine: my breathing and the breathing of the runners around me. Headphones just might block all of that out.

It might be possible to lull Puff back to sleep by running slowly before he finishes emptying your carb pantry. I think this is the thinking behind Jeff Galloway's Run Walk Method. The next time I sense Puff stirring, my strategy is to slow the heck down, and gradually, and I do mean ever so gradually, and ever so gently, speed up to as close as I can go to my desired pace without Puff opening his eyes again.

Two Thousand Miles

Running has become quite a passion for me and I've dedicated a lot of resources to it. It turns out that from April 2015 through May 2016 I ran an average of 5.6 miles a day or just over 2,000 miles! This is what the Garmin app shows in its annual summary view. I imported all the runs I did before buying my Garmin in October so it has data going all the way back to my first race of 2015, the BH5K. At an average of about 10 minutes a mile, this means I ran about 350 hours over one year. I run 6 days a week, and prep before, and shower after, takes about half an hour per day. This all adds another 150 hours a year totaling 500 hours a year dedicated to running. That's one fourth of a full time job spent running and I already have a full time job, two young adult kids a house and four pets to look after!

I expect to run a little less this coming season. I have a plan to prepare for the Freep International Half that calls for 40-ish miles a week which is considerably less than the 50 to 60 mile weeks required for marathon prep. Of course, when my prep for Boston kicks in, I'll be back to higher running volumes but for the next 5 months, I expect to have a break from trying to fit long distances into my busy schedule.

My spending on running was nothing to trifle with either. It turns out I spent over $2000 on running gear and proper clothing. I got a $130 dividend from REI for my spending in 2015 which means I spent $1300 there. At Hansons running, they checked how much I spent over that same period and it was close to $1300 as well. Most of what I spent at both stores was on running gear. I went from Rockports, cargo pants and cotton pocket tees to sophisticated base layers, polyester briefs, non-cotton tech shirts, and about a dozen pairs of running shoes. The shoes were definitely overkill but I do like being able to vary my shoes as a way to avoid repetitive motion injury. I have over 500 miles on my oldest pair of Ghost 6 GTXs and over 400 miles on my newer pair of Ghost 8 GTXs. Having almost half my miles concentrated on only two pairs of Gore Tex shoes is a testament to the slushy, messy, snowy and rainy conditions I ran in the winter of 2015-2016. And that was a mild winter!

I don't expect to spend nearly as much leading up to Boston. I now had a reliable running FR 235 watch and I even had a backup, unless I chose to sell the trusty FR 220 that got me through my first 3 marathons. I now had running shoes ranging from 0 drop to 14mm drop, ranging from light weight to heavy gore tex, ranging from cushioned to minimalist. I now had Smartwool and Arcteryx base layers. I now had polyester and spandex running shorts and tech shirts. I had fall and winter running jackets. I even had rainproof windproof breathable running attire.

So the only things I might need to buy going forward were replacements for shoes that would inevitably wear out. Running shoes typically are good for 400 miles. Some shoes you can spot wear right away. Others look fine but if you run in them you notice soreness. Listen to the soreness and replace them if they are high mileage shoes! I've had more than one runner tell me about injuries related to keeping shoes past their end of life. I donated a pair of 380 mile Glycerins to Hansons charity shoe recycling program. I didn't like the way they were wearing and I hated running in slippery conditions in the winter on those shoes. I don't think I'll opt for that shoe again because the sole design does not have good traction.

Conclusion

Running has become a great blessing in my life. I dabbled in running earlier in life but once I started running daily I found better physical, mental and spiritual health. Running isn't the most expensive hobby but picking up proper equipment to avoid injury is a lot less expensive than physical therapy to treat injuries received running without proper gear. I have found a community of support in my fellow runners. In just about one calendar year I went from jogging 3 miles to qualifying to run in the Boston marathon.

Running a marathon is more than a mere commitment to run 26.2 miles. It is really a commitment to run over 500 miles leading up to the marathon so you will be prepared to enjoy rather than suffer through your marathon. Qualifying for Boston is another level of commitment to achieve a particular time. This is what most often spoils a person's marathon experience, coming out too aggressively in order to meet a time goal for the race. I've learned that being well prepared and starting a marathon at a slower than goal pace and finishing with "negative splits" or at least no slower than you started can not only reduce fatigue and soreness but leave you with a feeling you haven't hardly run at all! I found the idea that running a certain way could leave a runner feeling refreshed at the end of a whopping 26.2 miles hard to believe as I was training for my BQ attempt but now that I've experienced it, I know it to be true.

The bottom line is this: Run for yourself. Running a particular pace or distance out of obligation to someone else will probably not lead to a pleasant experience. This is a hobby. Except for professional Olympic caliber runners, none of us are being paid for this. Run at your own pace. Try not to get sucked along by faster runners. Dawdling with slower runners and walkers can make for a pleasant easy run, but if you need a harder workout go for it.

Epilogue

I am busy at work on my second running book, which will probably be called, "Chasing Unicorns,

Journal of a Rookie Marathoner: Year 2." It will focus on my preparation for and my experience in the Boston Marathon in 2017. I visited www.baa.org to see when I'm eligible to sign up and I have to wait until the second week. It seems that beating my qualifying time by a mere four minutes thirty seconds doesn't allow me to register "early" so I'll be sitting there on September 19th at 10am with my mouse cursor hovering over the Boston Marathon registration link. If you want to follow my running before my next book comes out, check www.jeffruns.org for updates.

Thanks for following along with my running experience! I hope this book has helped inspire you to either take up running or continue running as it represents one of the most efficient exercises for fitness benefits. I've heard over the years how running can be so terribly hard on the body and should be avoided by older adults and yet I see people my age and older running marathons, ultras and triathlons. The key is to seek and listen to advice. Be coachable and your risk of injury goes down and your chance of success goes up.

Running References

Jack Daniels, *Daniels' Running Formula*, Third Edition, (Champaign: Human Kinetics, 2013).

Jeff Galloway, *The Run Walk Method* (Maidenhead: Meyer & Meyer Sport, 2013).

Luke Humphrey, *Hansons Marathon Method*, Second Edition (Boulder: Velo Press, 2016).

Meb Keflezighi, *Meb for Mortals*, (New York: Rodale, 2015)

https://hansonscoachingservices.com/
http://www.usatf.org/
http://www.runnersworld.com/
http://www.runningintheusa.com/
http://www.jeffruns.org/

General References

CS Lewis, *A Grief Observed*, (New York: Harper Collins Ebooks, 2009)

Helen Macdonald, *H is for Hawk*, (New York: Grove Press, 2014).

Thick Naht Nahn, *Peace is Every Breath*, (New York: Harper Collins Ebooks, 2011)

Robert Persig, *Zen and the Art of Motorcycle Maintenance*, (New York: Harper Collins Ebooks, 2009)

Jerry L. Sittser, *A Grace Disguised*, (Grand Rapids: Zondervan, 2004).

Marcus Zusak, *The Book Thief*, (New York: Knopf, 2005)

Acknowledgements

Special thanks to my proofreaders and commenters, especially Jeff Lyijnen, Joyce Nolden, Robin Price, Chris Kendall, and Liz Kendall. Thanks to Hansons coaches Luke Humphery, Katie Kellner and Dani Miller. Special thanks to Father Richard Cassidy without whose inspiration and encouragement I would have never run my first marathon. For decades my late wife Michele tried to convince me to write a book. There were so many times we were talking and she would say "Jeff, you should write a book about that." Running may have provided the topic for this book but Michele provided the encouragement.